EVIDENCING
CPD

A Guide to Building Your
Social Work Portfolio

D1420011

WITHDRAWN

LIVERPOOL JMU LIBRARY

3 1111 01500 8673

**CRITICAL
SKILLS FOR
SOCIAL WORK**

Other books in this series:

Anti-racism in Social Work Practice
Edited by Angie Bartoli   ISBN 978-1-909330-13-9

Mental Health and the Criminal Justice System
By Ian Cummins   ISBN 978-1-910391-90-7

*Modern Mental Health: Critical Perspectives on Psychiatric
Practice*
Edited by Steven Walker   ISBN 978-1-909330-53-5

Observing Children and Families: Beyond the Surface
By Gill Butler   ISBN 978-1-910391-62-4

Personal Safety for Social Workers and Health Professionals
By Brian Atkins   ISBN 978 -1-909330-33-7

Positive Social Work: The Essential Toolkit for NQSWs
By Julie Adams and Angie Sheard   ISBN 978-1-909330-05-4

*Practice Education in Social Work: Achieving Professional
Standards, 2nd ed*
By Pam Field, Cathie Jasper & Lesley Littler   ISBN 978-1-911106-10-4

Psychosocial and Relationship-based Practice
By Claudia Megele   ISBN 978-1-909682-97-9

Social Media and Social Work Education
Edited by Joanne Westwood   ISBN 978-1-909682-57-3

*Starting Social Work: Reflections of a Newly Qualified
Social Worker*
By Rebecca Joy Novell   ISBN 978-1-909682-09-2

The Critical Years:Child Development from Conception to Five
By Tim Gully   ISBN 978-1-909330-73-3

Understanding Substance Use: Policy and Practice
By Elaine Arnull   ISBN 978-1-909330-93-1

*What's Your Problem? Making sense of Social Policy and
the Policy Process*
By Stuart Connor   ISBN 978-1-909330-49-8

Titles are also available in a range of electronic formats. To order please go to our website
www.criticalpublishing.com or contact our distributor NBN International, 10 Thornbury Road,
Plymouth PL6 7PP, telephone 01752 202301 or email orders@nbninternational.com.

EVIDENCING
CPD

A Guide to Building Your Social Work Portfolio

Daisy Bogg & Maggie Challis

Second Edition

CRITICAL SKILLS FOR SOCIAL WORK

First published in 2016 by Critical Publishing Ltd

All rights reserved. No part of this publication may be reproduced, stored in a retrieval system, or transmitted in any form or by any means, electronic, mechanical, photocopying, recording or otherwise, without prior permission in writing from the publisher.

Copyright © 2016 Daisy Bogg and Maggie Challis

British Library Cataloguing in Publication Data
A CIP record for this book is available from the British Library

ISBN: 978-1-911106-14-2

This book is also available in the following e-book formats:
MOBI ISBN: 978-1-911106-15-9
EPUB ISBN: 978-1-911106-16-6
Adobe e-book ISBN: 978-1-911106-17-3

The rights of Daisy Bogg and Maggie Challis to be identified as the Authors of this work have been asserted by them in accordance with the Copyright, Design and Patents Act 1988.

Cover design by Out of House
Text design by Greensplash Limited
Project Management by Out of House Publishing
Printed and bound in Great Britain by TJ International, Padstow

Critical Publishing

152 Chester Road
Northwich
CW8 4AL

www.criticalpublishing.com

MIX
Paper from
responsible sources
FSC
www.fsc.org   FSC® C013056

Contents

List of figures, useful information and activities

Figures

Useful information and activities

Meet the authors

Daisy Bogg

Daisy has worked within mental health and addiction services for the last twenty years, both for the NHS and also for voluntary sector organisations, from practitioner to Executive Director of Social Care for an integrated mental health trust. She is a qualified and HCPC registered social worker and has spent a large part of her career working within integrated health and social care environments, providing and developing professional leadership and integrated service improvement.

She also holds the roles of ASYE Independent Chair for SE London ETF partnership, Co-Chair of the Social Perspectives Network and Visiting Fellow at Bournemouth University delivering a range of BIA programmes across the country. She was endorsed as an individual trainer by TCSW CPD endorsement scheme, as well as continuing to practice as an Approved Mental Health Professional and a Best Interest Assessor. Daisy is Professional Lead for the Social Work Resources project.

Maggie Challis

Maggie has had a long career in adult, further and higher education, working as a tutor, researcher, manager and national project leader. She has worked with a range of professions, including medicine, nursing, physiotherapy and social work. She has published widely on the Accreditation of Prior and Experiential Learning (APEL), work-based learning, person-centred learning and quality assurance in education, and has presented at conferences in places as diverse as Sweden, Israel, South Africa, Cameroon and the Czech Republic. She has been an institutional auditor for the Quality Assurance Agency (QAA) for Higher Education, and has been external examiner on a range of professional programmes in seven universities.

During the last year Maggie has worked with Save the Children to devise core competencies for child protection, and has continued to work as an Associate of DBC on contracts with DH and DfE.

List of acronyms

AMHP	Approved Mental Health Professional
APEL	Accreditation of Prior and Experiential Learning
ASYE	Assessed and Supported Year in Employment
BIA	Best Interest Assessor
CCETSW	Central Council for Education and Training in Social Work
CPD	continuing professional development
CPL	continuing professional learning
DCSF	Department for Children, Schools and Families
DH	Department of Health
GSCC	General Social Care Council
HCPC	Health & Care Professions Council
HEI	higher education institution
HPC	Health Professions Council
IfL	Institute for Learning
JISC	Joint Information Systems Committee
JUCSS	Joint University Council for Social Studies
JUCSWEC	Joint University Council Social Work Education Committee
KSS	Knowledge and Skills Statements
NQSW	Newly Qualified Social Worker
NVQ	National Vocational Qualification
PCF	Professional Capabilities Framework
PEP	Practice Educator Programme
PQ	post-qualifying
PREP	post-registration on-going education and practice
PRTL	post-registration training and learning
QAA	Quality Assurance Agency for Higher Education
SoPs	Standards of Proficiency
SWRB	Social Work Reform Board
SWTF	Social Work Task Force
TCSW	The College of Social Work

Introduction

In 2007, the tragic death of Baby Peter in Haringey sparked a huge review of the way social workers manage cases involving the abuse of children. Since then, the whole of social work education and development has been under considerable scrutiny in an attempt to raise standards and develop a consistent approach to social workers' qualifying education and continuing professional development (CPD).

Between 2010 and 2012, the Social Work Reform Board, made up of key stakeholders from across the sector, developed a range of products aimed at supporting social workers in practice. These were passed over to The College of Social Work (TCSW) in 2012 when it opened its doors to members.

The development of the Professional Capabilities Framework (PCF) came about partly in response to the lack of career pathways and agreed quality standards across the profession. The PCF represented a new way of looking at learning which meant a shift in social workers' practice and in how they document and evidence their continuing professional development activities.

Between 2012 and 2014 the PCF continued to develop, with a range of specialist capabilities, curriculum frameworks and position statements/papers issued by TCSW. These were all aimed at strengthening professional standards and expectations and promoting a positive public perception of social work in the full range of settings.

There then followed the appointment of two Chief Social Workers – one for children and families located, with the Department for Education (DfE), and one for adults, located with the Department of Health (DH). These roles, initially intended to promote social work within government and create a link to front line practice, have since developed into civil service advisor roles, and both offices have issued Knowledge and Skills Statements (KSS) setting out the minimum expectations of social workers in each area.

By 2015 it had become clear that social workers were not joining TCSW, and it was announced that the organisation was no longer financially viable, would receive no further government funding and was to close. At this point, the PCF was transferred to the British Association of Social Workers (BASW) who now own the framework on behalf of the profession.

There has been some confusion in the sector in relation to how the PCF and KSSs work together. The PCF forms the generic framework that all social workers, regardless of practice specialism need to demonstrate whereas each KSS provides detail for its specialist area, as is the case with other capability statements (for example the Approved Mental Health Professional (AMHP) competencies and the Best Interest Assessor (BIA) capabilities.

All of these changes put the onus on social workers to show how they are working to meet the standards set out in the various frameworks and to use these standards to guide their continuing professional development.

This book aims to provide a practical guide to evidencing CPD for social workers using a portfolio-based approach. There are activities, exercises and templates throughout each chapter which are designed to help you reflect on your own practice and start to develop a portfolio which reflects your current level of work and your development needs, and is underpinned by the PCF.

Chapter overview

Chapters 1 and 2 set out the background and principles of the PCF and social work CPD and how the KSS is being implemented to provide the detailed knowledge and skills for social workers practicing in different settings. The aim here is to help you understand the context in which you are working and encourage you to begin to conceptualise how a portfolio could be used to evidence and develop your capabilities, linked to your individual needs and the requirements of the KSS and the social work regulator.

Chapters 4 and 5 move on to consider how portfolios can be used to support your on-going learning, and provide a range of exercises, templates and suggestions about what could be included in your professional portfolio.

Chapters 6 and 7 focus on particular phases of a social work career, namely qualifying and Assessed and Supported Year in Employment (ASYE) stages, and then moving on to CPD and into the KSS and accreditation phases of development, using a portfolio to plan and guide your activities. Chapter 8 follows the theme of career stages and considers how to use a portfolio for career development purposes.

Finally, Chapter 9 looks at how a portfolio can be assessed, and provides a framework to help you think about how to design your own portfolio according to the assessment systems it is likely to be used for. We look in particular at the KSS, with a view to supporting the assessment and accreditation process for colleagues working with children and families.

Several appendices are also provided which include templates that you can use to help you reflect on your practice and that can then be included in your own portfolio as evidence of on-going CPD activity.

Portfolios, whether paper-based or electronic, have been shown to be one of the most effective ways both to guide your learning and evidence the subsequent outcomes. At its most basic, a portfolio (or e-portfolio) is a collection of information and evidence which you can use to demonstrate your development for a range of purposes, including your continuing registration. To get the best out of a portfolio approach, you will need to think about what you need it to do and how you can integrate it into your day-to-day practice. This book will help you to do that.

The decade from 2002 to 2012 saw some significant changes to social work education, training and professional development. The work of the Social Work Task Force (SWTF) and the Social Work Reform Board (SWRB), as well as the recommendations of the Munro Review (Munro and Great Britain Department for Education, 2011), the work of The College of Social Work and subsequent developments introduced by the Offices of the Chief Social Workers, have all contributed to the overhaul of social work at all levels.

This initial chapter provides an overview of the context of social work education, training and development in order to support practitioners to conceptualise their own continuing professional development (CPD) range of standards and requirements. Social work is a contextual profession and a portfolio approach will enable self-reflection and self-directed learning, but in order to make the most of your learning it is important to be aware of the frameworks in place and the desired outcomes of these in a practice context.

A brief history of social work education and learning in England

Social work has been through a number of changes and developments over recent years, with the qualification to practice and the legal right to use the title 'social worker' becoming subject to more robust regulation. This reflects how the profession has grown and changed, and the value placed upon the role over time. It can sometimes be the case that social workers themselves are not always fully aware of where we have come from or the learning that we have gained as a result.

The idea of formalised and quality assured social work education can be traced back to the First World War (1914–1918). At this time, England was experiencing a significant change of direction in terms of social welfare policy in response to being able to meet the needs of a population affected by war. Throughout this period, social work was moving away from a charitable pursuit into the realms of state provided welfare. In recognition of this shift, in 1918 the Joint University Council for Social Studies (JUCSS) was established with the aim of co-ordinating the work of social studies departments across England (Payne, 2005). This was later replaced by the Joint University Council Social Work Education Committee (JUCSWEC), which still exists today.

Over the next 50 years, the role of the social worker continued to develop. In hospitals, almoners were appointed to undertake assessments of need and eligibility for services, and psychiatric social workers were introduced to asylums to carry out social assessments. The diversity of social work roles that were being established meant that training was focused on the area of work rather than on a set of common skills, and social workers were often linked into health services. This situation added to the lack of a unified professional identity and there were wide variations in the training courses that were being developed to meet the range of needs arising from the work.

The Seebohm report

The 1968 Seebohm report marked a major change for social work both as a profession and also in terms of how training and education is used and valued. This review came about as a result of some very familiar concerns.

> » Increasing levels of juvenile delinquency.

> » The need for family services to help the most deprived.

> » Increasing numbers of older people.

> » Poor co-ordination of personal social services.

> » Inadequate training for social workers. (Dickens, 2011, pp 22–39)

Social services provision at this time was split across a range of different departments, with social workers employed in diverse contexts and locations. While there was a desire to bring together social workers into a common professional group, this was far from being achieved. The Seebohm report set out a vision for unified social services departments with a central co-ordinating role for social workers, and this provided an opportunity for social workers to come together in a more coherent way.

In 1971, the Central Council for Education and Training in Social Work (CCETSW) came into being to oversee standards of social work education. At this time social work was a certificated occupation with a number of recognised entry routes. Over the next 20 years, social work continued to see significant developments and the Diploma in Social Work was introduced in 1991 as the single entry route for new social workers. Throughout the 1990s, there was increasing political pressure to implement a registration system, particularly for social workers in children and family contexts.

Social work registration

The Care Standards Act 2000 was passed through Parliament partly as a result of the concerns to implement a registration system. This piece of legislation represented a landmark for social work as a recognised profession, and introduced two key changes that helped to set the stage for the reviews and reforms that have led us to where we are today. Firstly, it set out the scope and remit of a new organisation – the General Social Care Council (GSCC) – whose role it would be to regulate and register social workers and social work education, as well as taking on a broader remit to undertake the strategic development and promotion of the whole social care sector in England. Secondly, it introduced the requirement of professional registration of social workers across England.

The General Social Care Council (GSCC), was established in 2001. During its ten years in full operation, the GSCC developed a range of approaches to managing the initial training and CPD of social workers, and over this period the profession grew and developed into a degree-level registered profession with the title of social worker protected in law.

In 2003, the degree was introduced as the minimum qualification for social work. The GSCC then turned its attention to how social workers continued to develop and learn once they had achieved qualification. It developed a post-qualification framework of awards which relied on the provision of courses and programmes by higher education institutions. The minimum requirement for continued registration did not depend upon gaining these higher education awards, however. It rested instead on social workers undertaking a minimum of 15 days or 90 hours of post-registration training and learning (PRTL) activity over the three-year period of registration. The form of CPD was not prescribed and was in practice generally interpreted as participating in courses from which a certificate of attendance could be obtained. There was therefore something of a mismatch between the desired academic route to CPD implicit in the post-qualifying (PQ) framework, and the reality of what social workers actually did to continue their learning. The result was that there was no way the GSCC could determine through its PQ framework or registration requirements whether CPD activity was leading to any changes in practice or improvement to services beyond the self-assessed comment on the post-registration training and learning (PRTL) form which asked about the perceived impact of the listed activities.

Interest in social care and social work was high throughout the 2000s, with various reviews and recommendations in relation to social work standards and training being considered. One of the key developments was a review carried out by the Department of Health (DH) in 2006 titled *Options for Excellence,* which made several recommendations in relation to the introduction of the Newly Qualified Social Worker (NQSW) role, the importance of good supervision and the need for CPD opportunities.

The momentum for reform and improvement across social work continued to grow, and in February 2009 the SWTF was established by the DH and the then Department for Children, Schools and Families (DCSF). The social work functions of DCSF have since been transferred to the Department for Education (DfE). Membership of the SWTF was drawn from across the profession from front line social workers and educators to the most senior of senior leaders, based on the acknowledgement that the best way to implement profession-wide change would be to task the profession itself to identify and implement the appropriate standards. The remit of the group was:

to undertake a comprehensive review of frontline social work practice and to make recommendations for improvement and reform of the whole profession, across adult and children's services. (SWTF, 2009, p 13)

The SWTF delivered its final report in December 2009 and made 15 recommendations which have underpinned subsequent developments. The SWRB was established in early 2010 and replaced the SWTF, with a remit of making the recommendations a reality across the social work profession.

The GSCC closed in July 2012 and the regulation and registration of social workers passed to the Health Professions Council (HPC) (which became the Health & Care Professions Council (HCPC)), with standards for the profession becoming the responsibility of the newly established professional college: The College of Social Work (TCSW).

Useful **information**

1.1 Social Work Task Force recommendation for CPD

Continuing professional development

[The] creation of a more coherent and effective national framework for the continuing professional development of social workers, along with mechanisms to encourage a shift in culture which raises expectations of an entitlement to on-going learning and development. (SWTF, 2009, p 13)

Recent reforms: from the Social Work Task Force to the Professional Capabilities Framework and KSS

The Social Work Task Force (SWTF) was clear that both social workers and their employers needed to take responsibility for enhancing the quality of social work practice, and also that the way in which initial and continuing education was conceived and organised was not sufficient to meet the needs of the profession. It was this view of an inconsistent pattern of CPD that led the SWRB to develop the concept of the Professional Capabilities Framework (PCF) as a means of establishing the new and co-ordinated approach to CPD.

Under GSCC, social work was described and assessed in terms of competencies. This approach has its roots in the National Qualifications Framework (NCVQ, 1991), which described what workers in 11 occupational areas should know and be able to do. The competency approach has been criticised as a tool for assessing complex tasks and knowledge needed for professional work (Eraut, 1994), and risks reducing these complexities to a set of 'tick box' activities which are assessed largely by observation.

The GSCC closed in July 2012 and the regulation and registration of social workers passed to the Health Professions Council – which became the Health & Care Professions Council (HCPC) when it took on the registration of social workers – with standards for the profession becoming the responsibility of a professional college – The College of Social Work (TCSW).

The PCF represented a move away from a competence-based approach and uses instead the concept of 'capability'. This approach attempts to define and describe the things that social workers should know and be able to do across the full range of their professional lives, including such vital issues as the use of professional judgement and working with uncertainty.

The notion of capability is significant because, as Eraut (1994, p 203) indicates, *it implies that the individual has the necessary knowledge and skills to perform in a wider range of situations than those that are observed*. This includes the cognitive processes being used by the professional person, and also makes the assumption that the professional has or will acquire a knowledge base that will support future practice. Implicit in this approach is also an understanding that individuals will understand the role of their profession in relation to individuals, employing organisations and wider society. Capability is about knowledge in use, in context and integrated into practice.

None of this can be captured through an atomised approach to practice which defines the professionals' performance through a series of tasks and performance-related knowledge.

The PCF was designed to underpin all stages of a social worker's development, from initial entry to a qualifying programme through to senior levels of strategic manager and policy maker. A principal social worker is measured against the outcomes of the PCF as assiduously as a first-year student preparing to go out on placement. Entry, readiness to practise, placements and graduation are all framed by the professional capabilities of the PCF, and assessment of achievement will be made against those professional outcomes. This means that the learning and assessment methods have to be adapted to capture capability, not competence.

The SWRB's approach to CPD attempted to capture this change in what is meant by 'professional practice' by recognising that courses and conferences are not sufficient to ensure that capability is developed and that knowledge continues to be enhanced and integrated into practice.

Unfortunately, TCSW was short-lived and in July 2015 it closed its doors and its products were re-assigned: the PCF was rehomed with BASW (www.basw.co.uk/pcf/) and the resources produced by The College on behalf of the DfE and DH were transferred to Daisy Bogg Consultancy Ltd. These can be found on the Social Work Resources website (http://socialworkresources.org.uk/).

The Knowledge and Skills Statements (KSS) issued by the Chief Social Workers belong to the relevant government department, and are intended to provide additional detail in relation to social work practice in specific areas, and in the case of child and family social work, at specific levels – approved practitioner, practice supervisor and practice leader. These are the focus of current developments in statutory social work practice and will be considered in more detail in Chapter 3.

Further changes to qualifying education

In 2014/15 two reviews of social work education were published, one commissioned by the DfE and written by Sir Martin Narey, and one commissioned by the DH, written by Professor David Croisdale-Appleby. While not in complete agreement about what needed to be in place, both reports highlighted some significant failings in the way social workers are trained, educated and supported with post-qualification learning and development. In Children and Families, a new way of training was being developed; this included 'Frontline', a fast-track training scheme, aimed at high achieving graduates and born out of partnership between employers and higher education institutions.

This approach to training social workers was supported by the then minister of education, Michael Gove, and the DfE invested heavily in the scheme as a solution to some of the recruitment and quality difficulties being experienced in front-line services. The DH soon followed suit, and in 2015 the Think Ahead programme was launched – a fast-track route into mental health social work. Again, this scheme targets high achieving graduates and is based on a partnership between employers and an academic partner, in this case the University of York. Both of these developments have caused controversy across the sector, with mixed views as to the success of these schemes in improving learning. There have also been concerns raised that to remove social work education from universities may be the start of eroding the nature of the profession and creating a disconnect between practice on the ground and research in the universities. While it can be argued that this link is far from embedded in the current arrangements, the move to a work-based learning route to qualification may have some unintended consequences in the future.

Continuing professional development (CPD)

A summary of a new approach to CPD was produced by TCSW in 2012. It makes the following statements in relation to the new way of addressing CPD in the context of professional capability.

> » *The approach will be aligned with the relevant levels of the professional capabilities framework (PCF) and linked to the career structure.*

> » *Social workers will be supported by employers and expected to take professional responsibility for developing their skills to a high professional level, through undertaking learning and development activities over and above the core standards required for re-registration with HPC.*

> » *A wide range of learning and development activities should be promoted. Space for critical reflection, learning from others and opportunities for access to research should be valued alongside more structured training. There is an aspiration that social workers should have the opportunity to achieve post qualifying (PQ) awards at Masters' level through modular programmes.*

> » *Learning and development needs will be identified, planned for and monitored through annual appraisal cycles and supervision.*

> » *Mechanisms for recognising and recording CPD activities will be established to provide clarity of process, and portability across the country.*

> » *Employers will be encouraged to develop learning opportunities working in partnership with other local employers and HEIs.* (TCSW, 2012c)

Although TCSW has now closed, the principles underpinning CPD that it produced continue to guide social workers' professional development.

This outline of a way of conceptualising CPD has implicit in it all the approaches to learning that are supported by a portfolio-based methodology where learning activity is planned in relation to specific identified need, is recorded, reflected upon, and then becomes the basis for future learning.

HCPC requirements for continued registration

One of the key changes that a change in regulator has brought is the approach to recording and evidencing CPD and on-going professional learning. Under GSCC regulation, social workers were required to undertake a minimum of 90 hours of PRTL over a three-year registration period. The HCPC has a very different approach. Gone is the required number of hours of activity, to be replaced by a process that looks at learning and impact, or outcomes as a result of that learning.

The HCPC audits 2.5 per cent of social workers at the end of each two-year registration period with the aim of monitoring that effective CPD is being undertaken. These audits started in 2014, and will be repeated in 2016. Social workers chosen for audit will be required to provide a CPD profile showing how they meet the required standards. These requirements are explored further in Chapter 6.

Reflective **activity**

1.2 Your current approach to CPD

Think about how you have previously kept records of your CPD activity and consider the following:

> » If you are one of the 2.5 per cent selected for audit today, what would you be able to provide as evidence for your registration?

> » Is the evidence you could provide for audit sufficient to meet the basic standards for CPD?

> » Is the evidence you could provide for audit doing justice to your professional practice capabilities?

> » What benefits could you see of keeping an on-going professional portfolio?

The next phase of reform

While the HCPC remains the regulator for social work professionals, at the time of writing this edition of Evidencing CPD an announcement was made in March 2016 by the Secretary of State for Education, Nicky Morgan, that by 2020 a new social work regulation body would be in place, taking over the role of the HCPC. This announcement came at the same time that the DfE and Chief Social Worker Office (Children and Families) are trialling an assessment and accreditation system for children and families social workers which will involve practitioners passing an online and practice simulation test to achieve the status of Approved Child & Family Social Worker (ACFSW).

Whether adult social workers will follow suit and move towards an accreditation system is not yet known. However, what we do know is that social work reform is continuing at a pace. In the absence of a professional college, social workers in all fields will need to make sure they keep up to date and are able to input into the continuing developments which shape the profession and the way it approaches CPD.

Chapter **summary**

This chapter has considered the history and development of social work professional development which has led us to where we are today. Social work reforms have been implemented at a rapid rate, and from the introduction of registration during 2003 and 2004 (from April 2005, social workers could not be employed unless registered; from September 2004, independent reviewing officers employed by local authorities could not be employed unless registered), we have now moved to a different regulatory body, established for a brief period our own professional college, and developed a capabilities framework that can be used by all social workers regardless of their specialist area or level of seniority.

The way we think about CPD has also seen some significant changes, and the new requirements make it increasingly important for practitioners to keep track of their CPD activities and learn how to evidence effectively their own learning. The KSS and the forthcoming assessment and accreditation system in children and families social work represent the next stage of reform, and portfolios, whether in paper copy or on an electronic platform offer an on-going learning opportunity for social workers as well as being a means for organising and storing their evidence to show that they meet the required standards.

While an appreciation of where we have come from is important, the focus of this book is how to create and use a portfolio to its best advantage, and consequently we must now move on to more practical matters. The PCF has become the standard for social work learning and should be the starting point for professional development activities, with the KSS providing the detailed descriptors of the required knowledge and skills. The next chapter will explore these frameworks and think about how a portfolio approach can be used both to provide evidence and to reflect on individual activities.

Chapter 2 | The Professional Capabilities Framework

So far, this book has provided an overview of the reforms to social work education and practice that have been developed and introduced since 2008. This includes the introduction of the Professional Capabilities Framework (PCF), which provides a common mechanism by which social workers at all levels and in the full range of practice areas should be planning and undertaking their continuing professional development (CPD).

This chapter considers the structure and levels of the PCF, and will support you in applying your own learning and developing your own portfolio in a way that helps you to evidence and continue to plan your CPD against the required standards and capabilities. The PCF is a significant professional change in terms of how social work is taught, developed and conceived, and practitioners need a thorough understanding of the requirements of the PCF in order to apply these to their own professional development activities (see Figure 2.1).

Useful **information**

2.1 PCF

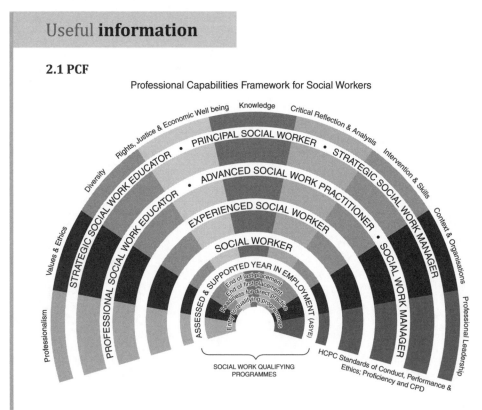

Professional Capabilities Framework for Social Workers

Source: © TCSW, 2012

Since the closure of TCSW in 2015, the PCF has been transferred to BASW and a review of the framework has been concluded. It is proposed that some refinements should be made to the descriptors, specifically in relation to the promotion of the level descriptors and further clarification of domain 9, professional leadership.

For more information, visit the BASW website at www.basw.co.uk/pcf.

Social work career levels and development pathways

One of the key recommendations of the Social Work Task Force (SWTF) was the development of a career framework for social work which included enabling practitioners to stay in practice and still develop their career (SWTF, 2009, Recommendations 9 and 10).

The Task Force noted that at the time of the review there was *no recognised progression route for keeping experienced, effective professionals in frontline practice* (SWTF, 2009, p 39), and set out a system, similar to those seen in other professions such as nursing and teaching, which enabled social workers to develop both their skills and their careers while remaining connected to front line practice.

The PCF embodies the recognition of a progression route and sets out career pathways that encompass practice, leadership and management, and academic education, setting the standards that would be expected of social workers as they progress through their respective career pathways.

Career levels and using portfolios

Regardless of what career level you are at (or on which development pathway), a portfolio may either be a requirement or simply a useful way to guide and keep track of your own CPD and learning. Reflection and critical analysis of practice are the key components of a good portfolio, and while it can seem like a time-consuming task when you first set out, once established it can serve as a source of focus, a means of monitoring progress, and evidence to support your on-going professional registrations and roles.

For more information about the roles within the KSS for child and family social workers and how the PCF and KSS can work together, see Chapter 3.

> ## Reflective **activity**
>
> **2.2 Why use a portfolio?**
>
> Whether keeping a portfolio is a requirement or simply one of the options you are considering, it is useful to understand the purpose that your portfolio serves in terms of supporting your own career development in the context of the PCF framework.
>
> The different functions that a portfolio can serve will be considered in more detail in Chapters 3 and 4, but for now it will be helpful to consider the following questions on how a portfolio approach might be beneficial to your career development pathway.
>
> » What are your overall CPD goals?
>
> » What do you need to do to reach your goals?
>
> » What do you need to demonstrate?
>
> » Who do you need to demonstrate CPD to?
>
> » In what ways can you demonstrate and evidence CPD?
>
> » How could a portfolio help you to evidence CPD?

The PCF recognises and sets out several levels from pre-qualifying through to senior roles which set the standards for continuing social work practice. These levels are separated into student, social work in practice, and advanced roles. Each level provides the foundation for the next progression. This means you can maintain and build a portfolio throughout your career which demonstrates your development against the nine domains in a logical and structured way. The specific career levels are detailed in the following sections.

Student social workers

For most social work students, portfolios will become second nature. Your placements and supervision will be focused on developing evidence of capability against the PCF domains and students will develop a portfolio as part of the assessment process used by their university course (TCSW, 2012a). As a student, there are four levels to work through, from entry to qualification, and these are designed to equip you with the skills and knowledge that you will need to move into your first qualified social work role. They include the following:

Entry – includes the capabilities that are expected of an individual entering social work qualifying programmes. There is a range of personal qualities that all social workers require, and an awareness of social context and the impact this can have are essential prerequisites for undertaking training to be a professional social worker.

Readiness for direct practice – includes the capabilities that are expected of social work students about to undertake their first placements, and include areas such as communication, working with people, working within an organisation and the core social work values. Students need to demonstrate that they have this basic level of skill prior to engaging in their placements and undertaking direct work with vulnerable individuals under supervision.

The end of the first placement – includes the capabilities that are expected of a social work student completing placement. These include the application of knowledge, skills and values and being able to show that you have the ability to work with people in complex situations with supervision and support.

The end of the qualifying programme – includes the capabilities that are expected of a newly qualified social worker. These are designed to demonstrate a foundation level of capability across all areas and form the starting point for CPD activities. Once qualified, you will be able to register with the Health & Care Professions Council (HCPC) as a social worker in England; you will need to do this to be able to practise and call yourself a social worker.

Social worker and experienced social worker

Once you are qualified, there is an expectation that, whatever role you undertake, there will be an opportunity to engage in CPD activity. This should help you both to extend your skills, knowledge and capability and to ensure that you stay up to date with the latest evidence and continue to improve and develop your practice. Within the areas of social worker and experienced social worker, there are three levels (TCSW, 2012a), which are detailed in the following sections.

Assessed and Supported Year in Employment

The Assessed and Supported Year in Employment (ASYE) replaces the previous Newly Qualified Social Worker (NQSW) scheme and is based on the Task Force recommendation of support and assessment in the first employed social work role. While not all organisations will offer an ASYE programme, there is still an expectation that your CPD activities will be focused on helping you to build your professional confidence and capability (TCSW, 2012b). Reflection and supervision are core aspects of this level of the PCF and social workers are expected to seek (and receive) appropriate support as well as evaluate and take a critical view of their own practice and learning. For readers at the ASYE career level, a range of resources is available from Skills for Care that can be drawn on and used as sources of evidence within your own portfolio. These can be found at www.skillsforcare.org.uk/social-work/introductionsw.aspx.

If you are working in an adult social work setting, you will also need to demon-strate the level of capability set out in the Knowledge and Skills Statement (KSS); Chapter 3 considers these requirements in more detail.

As an ASYE candidate, it is likely that you will be required to keep a portfolio to help you evidence your capabilities throughout your particular programme. However, for those not employed by an organisation that provides a formal ASYE scheme, and for social workers beyond the first year of practice, there may not be a formal require-ment to maintain a portfolio approach to your CPD. You may nevertheless find it to be a helpful way to demonstrate your continuing and developing capabilities, and for collating evidence to support your continued registration as a social worker.

Social worker role

As you progress in your career as a social worker, you are expected to have the cap-abilities to practise effectively, make complex decisions and respond to the context in which you work. The capabilities at this level set out the knowledge, skills and pro-fessional development standards which should be applied to your particular area of expertise and practice.

Experienced social worker role

For those with more experience, there is a higher expectation of the expertise and effectiveness of practice, managing higher levels of risks and providing supervision and leadership to colleagues and accountability for the practice of others. The capabilities at this level set out the standards expected by the profession for practice at this level.

Advanced level

As social workers move into more senior posts, there has traditionally been a lack of emphasis on their social work skills and capabilities and more focus on management and leadership skills and knowledge.

The advanced levels of the PCF attempt to address this gap and link management, leadership, education and practice skills into the framework, allowing social workers to develop and demonstrate their capabilities in a more holistic way. This recognises that practice occurs in a range of contexts, and that the capabilities and development needs of practitioners at advanced levels should still be appropriately prioritised by both social workers and their employers. These social workers are responsible for leading, educating and supporting others in practice and need to be able to model good practice to others. As such, they also need to remain reflective and critical practitioners who can draw on evidence, operate within context and maximise the social work contribution to improving outcomes. There are three pathways within this career level (TCSW, 2012d, 2012g), which are detailed in the following sections.

Advanced social work practitioners

The capabilities in this pathway support social workers who continue to work directly with people who use services, as well as providing leadership and professional guidance and consultation to colleagues. The capabilities aim to support constructive challenge to improve both practice and service delivery and emphasise the use of evidence-based practice and critical reasoning as would be expected of a practice leader.

Professional social work educators

Many social workers are involved in education, including practice educators and supervisors, researchers and teachers within university and other settings contributing to teaching, curriculum development and assessment approaches, trainers providing quality CPD programmes for social workers in practice, and those in learning and development roles with a responsibility for developing CPD programmes across the workforce. The capabilities of these practitioners will have a direct impact on the practice of others and they are expected to take a lead role in modelling good practice in relation to their own career development.

Social work managers

Managers are expected to *lead, motivate, nurture and manage* (TCSW, 2012b, p 1), and the capabilities in this pathway focus on supporting quality practice through managing performance, quality and partnerships. As with the other pathways within the advanced career level, social work managers are expected to model best practice and are accountable for the practice of others. Consequently, both social work managers and their employers need to place appropriate priority on their own career development.

Strategic level

Practitioners operating at this level, particularly within an organisational, regional or national context, may feel that their own CPD and career development has moved away from social work and is far more appropriately located within the sphere of politics, policy and leadership. This career level within the PCF recognises these skills but firmly links them back into social work core values and capabilities, enabling leaders to relate their roles more effectively to the values of the profession. Practitioners at this level are able to influence and shape standards and expectations, they are accountable for resources and outcomes and make strategic decisions that may affect a range of groups, communities or society. There are three pathways within this final level which are designed to support strategic leaders to consider their own development needs within the context of the profession and to set the standard of what is expected of social workers operating at this level (TCSW, 2012e). These pathways are detailed in the following sections.

Strategic social work educators

Social work educators at this level in their careers are responsible for responding to professional needs across the range of areas, including policy, partnerships and changes in law and evidence. They lead change management within the context of social work education and take a strategic approach to ensuring that education, research and/or learning delivers the desired outcomes for service users and other stakeholders, is rooted in best practice and is underpinned by robust quality assurance mechanisms and support structures. The capabilities expected of a social worker within this type of role are complex and multifaceted but are underpinned by the same PCF domains as other roles.

Principal social workers

The principal social worker role was introduced as a result of recommendations made in the Munro report (Munro and Great Britain Department for Education, 2011, Recommendation 14). The role is designed to be a senior manager who retains responsibility for practice with a local authority child and family setting both to support and represent the views of front line staff at management level. The capabilities expected in this career pathway are focused on how practice can inform and influence at various organisational levels, and social workers within these roles are expected to be able to manage competing demands, represent professional issues, influence systems and organisations and model good practice on an organisation-wide level (TCSW, 2012e).

Since the publication of the first edition of this book, the principal social worker role has been further developed and two national networks established – the Adult PSW Network and the Principal Child and Family Social Worker (PCFSW) Network. These forums have provided an opportunity for sharing learning across organisations and the process of evaluating the impact of the role within Local Authorities has begun, with evidence of increased quality assurance and focus on practice in organisations where the role is well embedded. More information about the PSW networks is available at www.socialworkresources.org.uk.

Strategic social work managers

Social workers within this pathway are likely to be skilled senior managers and leaders working at local, regional or national levels. They work across the full range of stakeholder groups and are responsible for delivering service change and quality improvements (TCSW, 2012e). As with other managers, they are responsible for leading, motivating and managing but they are expected to develop the capabilities to influence on a more strategic level and lead the consideration of *equalities, inclusion and diversity in strategic decision making* (TCSW, 2012e, p 4).

Reflective **activity**

2.3 Identifying your career level

While some readers may already have a defined career level, for others this may not be clear-cut. Where the latter is the case, it will be helpful for you to consider the following questions in order to identify the career level and, at the more advanced stages, the development pathway most appropriate to your goals and aspirations.

» What groups do you most frequently have contact with in the course of your practice? Eg service users and carers, colleagues, students, communities.

> » What is your main function in your day-to-day role? Eg support service users, support practitioners, deliver services, research evidence, teach.
>
> » What are you trying to achieve in your day-to-day practice?
>
> » Do you have responsibility for the practice of others?
>
> » What level of influence do you have on practice, standards, organisational policies and national policies?
>
> Re-read the descriptions provided in this chapter. Which level and pathway describes most closely the answers you have just given?

The PCF domains

Regardless of when you undertook your social work training, your current career level or which development pathway you are following, the nine domains within the PCF will not be new to you. They are based on the core social work values and skills that should be very familiar to most social workers.

The domains set out the capabilities that social workers are expected to meet at each career level, and these are designed to build upon each other to increase and expand your skills and knowledge as you progress and develop your practice. The nine domains overlap, and you will find that some of the evidence in your CPD portfolio will help to show your capabilities in a number of domains.

Each domain sets out what is expected of a professional social worker, and includes a range of detailed capabilities in each area to work through. A portfolio approach will help you to see how the capabilities build upon each other and to identify any development needs or gaps in evidence that you may have. The following box sets out the nine domains and an overview of what is included; in Appendix 1 these are broken down into the specific capabilities to help you to think about how you might apply these to your CPD.

Useful **information**

2.4 PCF domains and overarching statements

Domain	Overarching statement
Professionalism	Identify and behave as a professional social worker, committed to professional development.
Values and ethics	Apply social work ethical principles and values to guide professional practice.
Diversity	Recognise diversity and apply anti-discriminatory and anti-oppressive principles in practice.
Rights, justice and economic wellbeing	Advance human rights and promote social justice and economic wellbeing.
Knowledge	Apply knowledge of social sciences, law and social work practice theory.
Critical reflection and analysis	Apply critical reflection and analysis to inform and provide a rationale for professional decision making.
Intervention and skills	Use judgement and authority to intervene with individuals, families and communities to promote independence, provide support and prevent harm, neglect and abuse.
Contexts and organisations	Engage with, inform and adapt to changing contexts that shape practice. Operate effectively within one's own organisational frameworks and contribute to the development of services and organisations. Operate effectively within multi-agency and inter-professional settings.
Professional leadership	Take responsibility for the professional learning and development of others through supervision, mentoring, assessing, research, teaching, leadership and management.

A summary of the capabilities within each domain is provided in Appendix 1. Full details of the PCF can be found on the webpages of BASW (www.basw.co.uk/pcf).

Each domain contains a range of capabilities. These become increasingly complex and require more autonomous action and decision making as you progress through your social work career. Re-registration, on-going CPD and in some contexts career progression with employers will be based upon social workers' ability to demonstrate their capabilities against the PCF framework. Training, supervision and other development activities should be focused upon social workers' developmental needs within this context.

A review of the PCF, concluded in 2015, recommended that domain 9 should be further refined to move beyond an education and teaching emphasis and towards a practice leadership focus. BASW have stated an intention to accept this recommendation and some refinements will be made to this domain in 2016/17. Visit the BASW website for more information: www.basw.co.uk/pcf/review2015.

A portfolio approach to PCF domains

Analysing, demonstrating and evidencing the full range of capabilities and ensuring that CPD activities are focused on improving practice can be a complex task. Taking a portfolio approach, with a central point to collect, monitor, analyse and reflect on your learning and developmental needs, can provide a useful overview of all the available evidence and activities you are engaged in, with tools such as reflective logs serving as a way to consider how practice has been impacted as a result of your own critical appraisals. (Useful tools that can be used to help you to develop your portfolio will be considered in more detail in Chapter 4 of this book.)

Your portfolio might include evidence of training courses you have participated in, other learning opportunities, reading, research, reflections on incidents at work or effectiveness of interventions, supervision meetings or other reflections on activities that you have been engaged in within your role. Over the course of a relatively short period, you may end up with many pieces of evidence that, viewed as a collection of information, say little about the impact this activity has had or how you have used it to inform and improve your practice. The PCF sets out the standards which you are expected to meet, and your portfolio should be structured so that you can clearly see which capabilities each activity relates to and how your learning supports your on-going CPD plans and goals.

Reflective **activity**

2.5 Using the PCF to structure your portfolio

Think about a recent training or supervision experience where you reflected and analysed your practice and identified a learning point. Now answer the following questions.

» Which PCF domain(s) does your learning apply to? (It may cross more than one domain, depending on the experience you are reflecting on.)

» Which capabilities within the identified domain(s) does your learning apply to? (Again, this may include multiple capabilities.)

» How will your learning change or improve your practice?

» What benefit does your learning and the subsequent impact on practice have for you, your service users, those you supervise or other social work policies or practices?

» How does you evidence these improvements and outcomes?

Your answers in this activity help you to map your learning to the relevant PCF capabilities and to consider the impact of learning on practice. However you record your answers, they can be used to evidence both your understanding of the PCF and demonstrate how it applies to your practice. They will also help you to think through how best to evidence your overall CPD and application of critical social work practice.

Chapter **summary**

This chapter has set out the levels, pathways and domains within the PCF and considered how a portfolio approach can be used both to develop your capabilities and to form a coherent record of your professional development against the expected standards of the profession. The specific capabilities you are working on or towards will vary according to your own context and the types of activity you are engaged in. However, regardless of this, a portfolio can be a helpful way for you to manage your own CPD plans and learning goals as well as providing evidence to others (for example, supervisors, assessors) that you are applying the required standards and taking responsibility for your own development needs as a professional practitioner. The rest of this book will support you to develop a portfolio that meets your specific needs, including a range of activities, exercises and tools that can be incorporated into your portfolio, and it will continue to consider how the PCF can be used to inform learning and improve practice in the whole range of social work settings and contexts.

The establishment of the two Chief Social Worker roles and offices has led to further developments, as the reform programme moves on from the initial work of the reform board, and the government attempts to establish consistent standards in both adult, and children and family social work practice.

While many social workers will now be familiar with the PCF, its domains, levels and assessment methodologies, the Knowledge and Skills Statements are currently less well known but are being used to underpin the next stage of reform.

Children and families social workers

Since the publication of Sir Martin Narey's report into social work education, the DfE and the Chief Social Workers' Office for Children and Families have introduced and/ or announced some significant developments, including an assessment and accreditation scheme and the introduction of an approved practitioner status that is achieved through this scheme. They have also produced KSS for supervisors and practice leaders, which set the standard across social work with children and families. It is not confirmed at the moment whether this, too, will be assessed through a national scheme.

Assessment and accreditation scheme

Approved Child & Family Practitioner (ACFP)

Within the social work KSS, children and family practitioners should have knowledge and skills in a number of areas; these will be tested by computer-based examination and practice simulation assessment exercises. It has been announced that this will be in place nationally by 2020 and is currently in the testing phase at the time of writing the second edition of this book.

The knowledge and skills identified are listed in full in Appendix 2. These include:

> » Child development, including the ability to critically evaluate theory and research findings and demonstrate evidence-informed practice.

> » Adult mental ill-health, substance misuse, domestic violence, physical ill-health and disability, including being able to identify and respond to the impact these factors can have on a family and the wellbeing of both children and adult family members.

» Abuse and neglect of children, including being able to recognise and respond to risk indicators for different sorts of harm.

» Effective direct work with children and families (it was recognised in the Munro report (2011) that direct interaction between social workers and children and families is an important element of practice and is a skill that should be developed).

» Child and family assessment, including in-depth and ongoing assessments of need, risk, social functioning, parenting capacity and capability for change.

» Analysis, decision making, planning and review, focusing on developing critical skills and using these to develop and test hypotheses, apply theoretical understandings and research outcomes and demonstrate effective care planning as a result.

» The law and the family justice system recognises the importance of legal frameworks in the social work role and sets the expectation that practitioners are able to work within and negotiate the pathways and processes involved in child and family social care law and family justice proceedings.

» Professional ethics locates the knowledge and skills set out in the statement within the context of professional judgement and social work values, asking social workers to demonstrate their ability to balance complex and competing agendas while safeguarding the best interests of children.

» The role of supervision and research are emphasised as critical factors in the development of professional practice.

» Organisational context focuses on the contexts and settings of practice and the duties involved in the delivery of statutory activities.

Practice supervisor

Building on the knowledge and skills set out in the social worker KSS, the practice supervisor statement focuses on the knowledge and skills required of those that supervise, mentor and support frontline child and family social workers.

Practice leader

This KSS focuses on the strategic leaders within and across organisations. It recognises that solid frontline practice needs to be supported and quality assured. The developments in the role of the principal social worker (PSW) have in part influenced the development of this KSS level.

Adult social workers

Rather than identifying role levels as per the children and families KSS, the KSS for adult social workers, published in March 2015 (DH, 2015), sets out the expected level of capability for social workers at the end of their Assessed and Supported Year in Employment (ASYE) and specifies the roles and tasks expected of social workers practising with adults across the various service user groups.

Elements of the KSS

The adult KSS sets out ten core areas that social workers need to demonstrate. These are set out in full in Appendix 2, but in brief include the following areas:

»   Person-centred practice, which focuses on the views, wishes and experiences of the service user in their particular context.

»   Safeguarding, which details the expectations of a social worker in both preventative approaches and delivery of safeguarding enquiries under the Care Act 2014.

»   Mental Capacity is a significant practice focus for all adult social workers, and the KSS has specific guidance on what social workers should be skilled and knowledgeable about within this complex area of practice.

»   Effective assessments and outcome-based support planning are core functions of most social work roles and are highlighted as an essential skill for all practitioners.

»   Direct work with people emphasises the importance of developing and maintaining a 'toolkit' of interventions and is linked to domain 7 of the PCF.

»   Supervision, critical reflection and analysis seek to locate social work practice in evidence-informed approaches, and emphasise the importance of reflective practice.

»   Organisational context, focuses on the complex interrelationships social workers are required to maintain in order to effectively deliver their roles.

»   Professional ethics and leadership, provides detail of how social workers should advocate and lead within a value-based ethical framework.

Many of these areas overlap with PCF domains, and they should be viewed as a more detailed description of knowledge and skills expected for those who work within the field of adult social work.

Expectations at ASYE level

The adult KSS complements and builds upon the PCF descriptor and specifies tasks and roles in which a newly qualified social worker should be able to demonstrate capability at the end of their ASYE year. These include tasks such as:

» completing assessments of need;

» developing professional relationships;

» becoming more effective in their interventions;

» application of person-centred planning, risk assessment and risk management;

» confidence in working in multi-disciplinary settings;

» experience and skills in a particular service user group;

» maintaining and expressing a social work perspective;

» understanding and working with legislation;

» undertaking mental capacity assessments and working proactively in safeguarding situations;

» seeking supervision and engaging in reflective practice;

» caseload management and the demonstration of sound professional judgement (DH, 2015).

The full adult KSS is provided in the appendices of this book and is available from www.gov.uk/government/uploads/system/uploads/attachment_data/file/411957/KSS.pdf.

Chapter summary

This chapter has set out the key developments associated with the next stage of a continuing reform process, and the details included within the KSS. While the DH and DfE are currently taking different approaches regarding how to ensure social workers are maintaining practice standards, several developments have been carried out across the sector and it is likely that while the pathways may differ, each area impacts upon the other. Social workers will need to ensure they keep themselves up to date on the overall developments as well as in their own specific practice area.

Chapter 4 | What is portfolio-based learning?

Changes to social work education and continuing professional development (CPD) mean that as a profession we now need to think very differently about how we demonstrate on-going critical reflection and learning. The transfer of social work registration to the Health & Care Professions Council (HCPC) and the resulting shift in emphasis away from counting hours and towards reflection and impact in practice, mean that it is increasingly important that social workers are supported to develop and maintain an on-going collection of CPD evidence. One of the most effective and efficient ways of achieving this is by taking a portfolio-based approach to learning and development.

Portfolios are not new, but their use in initial and continuing professional development in social work is still in its relative infancy. This chapter aims to provide readers with an understanding of the evidence base to support portfolio-based learning, and how this can be applied within the context of professional social work.

What is a portfolio?

Portfolios are used across a whole range of sectors to support professional development and to evidence learning outcomes. For the purposes of clarity the definitions being used here are as follows.

A professional development portfolio is a collection of material, made by a professional, that records, and reflects on, key events and processes in that professional's career. (Hall, 1992, p 81)

[A] collection of material brought together for a specific purpose. (Challis, 1999, p 71)

In the past, portfolios would have been paper based. However, they are now increasingly electronic and there are many examples of online portfolios which are being used effectively to demonstrate a wide range of skills and knowledge across a range of professions.

The contents of a portfolio may be any information or evidence that shows how learning and development has been achieved, or how and why it is being planned. This may include video or audio recordings, objects or photographs, and a range of documents such as minutes of meetings or supervision sessions, critical incidents, case histories or reports, or online discussions and debates, as well as the more traditional certificates from training days. It is worth remembering, however, that a portfolio should not just be a random collection of material; it should be gathered together with a particular purpose in mind. That purpose may be to help personal reflection or it may be to demonstrate a particular piece of learning that has to be presented to another person for review and assessment. The different types of evidence will be explored in more detail in Chapter 4.

Why use a portfolio?

There is a whole range of purposes for a portfolio, and a comprehensive range of templates and structures in use. Some will be little more than a log book recording specific activities, while others will offer an in-depth and long-term perspective on professional development over an extended period.

Developing and maintaining a portfolio approach to professional development can be a daunting prospect, and having a desired outcome in mind prior to embarking on the task is important. Understanding what the portfolio needs to demonstrate will enable more effective planning and also serve to minimise the chances of it becoming nothing more than a chronological list of training courses attended in any given time period.

The following exercise is intended to help you to identify the purpose and desired outcomes of any portfolio activity you undertake.

Reflective **activity**

4.1 Identifying the goal of a portfolio

Consider the following questions. If you write down your answers you can use this as evidence in your portfolio of your own reflection and CPD.

» What do you need to demonstrate?

» Who do you need to demonstrate CPD to?

» Why do you need to demonstrate CPD?

» What type of evidence is needed?

» How does the evidence need to be presented?

» What is the goal of the portfolio?

» What other professional goals might the portfolio support?

Some additional things to think about include the following:

» Is the portfolio likely to be for your own private use or will someone else look at it? What difference does this make to what you might choose to include?

» Is the portfolio likely to be used for 'high stakes' assessment (eg so you can complete an educational assignment or re-register as a social worker) or is it for developmental purposes?

» Would you prefer to keep the portfolio electronically or as a paper-based document?

» Who can help you put your portfolio together?

Whatever the purpose behind the development of a portfolio, that purpose should be clear and understood by both the owner and any person who will be making judgements based on its contents. Portfolios are normally integrally related to a personal or professional learning plan. This forms the framework within which portfolio development takes place, and provides a statement of the outcomes which the portfolio seeks to demonstrate. For social workers, this framework is likely to be the Professional Capabilities Framework (PCF), as explored in Chapter 2 or one of the KSS, as explored in Chapter 3.

What is the educational rationale for using portfolios?

This book is concerned with the professional development of social workers. From the time they enter university programmes, social work students are, in psychological terms, adults. That is to say, they have passed the stage of formal operations which Piaget and colleagues (Piaget et al., 1929) believed was attained during adolescence and which he felt represented the culmination of cognitive development.

Psychologists exploring the subject of adult learning in the 1970s began to uncover aspects of adult cognitive development that have since had a bearing on the teaching and facilitation of learning in adults. Riegel (1973) suggests that learning is influenced by adults' ability to use dialectical logic, based on principles of working with contradiction, and the ability to identify problems or pose questions. He also proposes that a significant feature of adult thinking is the ability to reunite the abstract and the concrete, and thus explore complex problems.

If this is the case, then a model of education which is based on a didactic, teacher-led approach, as has traditionally been the case in higher education, may deny adult learners the opportunity to use or develop their full potential. It presents a 'handed-down' interpretation of reality for acceptance, rather than giving the learners the opportunity to define, explore or even create their own reality.

Riegel's view may be seen to be in line with the proposal made by Knowles (1970), where he presents a model that shows the distinctiveness of adult learning in four key areas.

1. As a person matures, there is a shift away from a self-concept of a dependent personality, towards one which is self-directed.

2. Accumulated experience becomes a resource for learning.

3. Readiness to learn becomes increasingly orientated towards the developmental tasks of social roles.

4. Time perspectives change from one of postponed application of knowledge to immediacy of application – thus learning moves from being subject-centred to problem-centred.

The implications of accepting these characteristics of adult learning are significant in terms of considering how professionals in training might most effectively engage in their own learning and development. The new model of delivering qualifying programmes in social work, which rests on a significant amount of time spent in practice and focuses on group work and problem-based approaches to learning, should encourage learning which will enable graduates to continue to use these approaches for their future professional development.

Knowles expanded some of these implications in terms of appropriate models for the facilitation of learning (Knowles, 1970). These include aspects such as the learning climate, diagnosis of needs, the planning process, conduct of the learning experience and evaluation of learning. Central to each of these is the fact that adults enter into any undertaking with a background of experience and learning from that experience. Therefore, teaching (or facilitating) techniques that build on experiential learning may be perceived by the learners as an extension of everyday life, and will be based on the assumption that learning from experience is as valid as other forms of learning. The trend to introduce problem-based learning into a range of programmes is founded on these assumptions.

However, there also exists a model of initial and continuing professional development which is based on a pattern of attendance at lectures or workshops, and a requirement to engage in such activities for a specified number of hours, rather than on an identifiable increase in learning. The General Social Care Council's (GSCC) post-registration training and learning (PRTL) requirements were an example of such an approach, and set out the requirement that:

Every social worker registered with the GSCC shall, within the period of registration, complete either 90 hours or 15 days of study, training, courses, seminars, reading, teaching or other activities which could reasonably be expected to advance the social worker's professional development or contribute to the profession as a whole. (GSCC, 2005)

Under these circumstances of 'counting hours' rather than measuring learning, there is a risk that the learner continues to be seen as dependent, participating in someone else's agenda of desirable learning. Individual histories and experiences of the learners are not embedded in the facilitative process, and application of the anticipated new learning is not necessarily related to the everyday roles of the participants and is necessarily deferred.

Knowles' work resonates with the notions of deep and surface learning originally developed by Marton and Saljo (1984) and subsequently developed by Gibbs (1992). Gibbs contends that the quality of the outcome of learning is crucially affected by the way in which individuals approach their learning. Gibbs describes the key characteristics of a model of facilitating learning, which leads to a 'deep', as distinct from a 'surface', approach to learning. These characteristics are those:

» which recognise that a learner's motivation is intrinsic, and they experience a need to know something;

» where learners are actively involved in their own learning, rather than a passive recipient;

» where there are opportunities for exploratory talk and interaction with others;

» where knowledge is approached as a series of integrated wholes, and related to other knowledge, rather than presented in small separate pieces.

Portfolio-based learning encapsulates these principles of adult learning, and at the same time offers an effective means of not only facilitating and recording development activities and valuing the individual's unique experiences, but also a means of reviewing and assessing that learning. Portfolios may also contribute to and enhance professional dialogue and collaboration within the CPD and reflective learning processes of the individual practitioner.

> ## Practice **example**
>
> ### 4.2 Blogging for collaboration and CPD
>
> Work undertaken by Tosh and Werdmuller in 2004 identified the potential benefits of blogs used in connection with e-portfolios. For those who benefit from online learning approaches, blogs lend themselves to collaborative learning. Returning to the blog to see how it has been received can prove motivational, and the process also allows for evaluative or reflective activity through a review of cumulative postings.
>
> Blogging can also provide an environment in which to explore the relationship between theoretical knowledge and other life and learning experiences. The dialogue that is entailed in the blog enables learners to gain a clearer vision, not only of the immediate demands of the curriculum or subject under discussion, but potentially of their future career development. All of this activity can be recorded in a portfolio, and used to demonstrate how learning has been acquired and used.

What are the benefits of a portfolio approach?

There are many benefits that arise from the use of portfolio-based learning that may not exist in other forms of educational activity or professional support. For example, portfolio-based learning:

- » recognises and encourages the autonomous and critically reflective learning that is an integral part of professional education and development;
- » is based in the real experience of the owner, and so enables the consolidation of the connection between theory and practice;
- » allows a range of learning styles to be used according to the preferences of the owner;
- » enables assessment within a framework of transparent and declared criteria and learning objectives;
- » can accommodate evidence of learning from a range of different contexts and over a period of time;

» provides a process for both formative and summative assessment based on learning outcomes which have either been developed by the owner or stipulated by an external agency;

» provides a model for lifelong learning and CPD based on critical reflection.

Keeping a portfolio of work is nothing new: architects, artists and writers have been doing it for years. Such portfolios are generally maintained in order to demonstrate achievement to someone who is in a position to make a judgement on its contents. The portfolio itself may be generic, consisting of a very large collection of items, or it may be specific, drawing upon selections of evidence designed to suit the purpose for which they are to be used. It may be developed and evaluated within strictly defined and pre-specified criteria, or it may be developed largely according to the purposes and progression of the individual learner. The portfolio may also be personal or professional, private or public, externally evaluated or assessed, or for individual reflection only (Challis, 1993).

What is the experience of other professional groups?

Portfolio-based learning has been introduced successfully into a range of educational and professional learning contexts. This may have been prompted largely in the UK by the move towards competence-based assessment and the introduction of National Vocational Qualifications (NVQs), where the emphasis is on evidence of achievement rather than on the educational processes undertaken by the learner (Simosko, 1991; Redman, 1994). Within this framework, the portfolio is designed to demonstrate how the learner has met the outcomes that form the basis of the qualification. An example of this in social work can be found in the National Occupational Standards for social work which, immediately prior to the PCF being implemented, underpinned the social work curriculum and are evidenced through practice placement. Similarly, the Newly Qualified Social Worker (NQSW) competences, which pre-dated the reforms to social work education introduced in 2012, were based on occupational standards which derive from the NVQ approach.

The use of portfolios as a tool for development in initial and continuing professional development, taking into account process as well as outcome, has grown over the years. The Nursing and Midwifery Council, for example, uses a 'professional profile' as part of its post-registration on-going education and practice (PREP) requirements (NMC, 2012). The purpose of this profile is to help nurses to plan and implement their

CPD by keeping records of educational activity and so encourage the development of critical and reflective practice.

Teachers in training, both in schools and higher education institutions (HEIs), are encouraged to maintain portfolios that demonstrate the development of their teaching skills (Graham, 1989). Within medical education too, the value of portfolio development is becoming recognised and portfolios are now used by both junior doctors and experienced doctors to demonstrate and plan their learning (Driessen, 2008).

For example, General Practitioners are required to use the Royal College of General Practitioners e-portfolio to present evidence of CPD for both appraisal and revalidation purposes (www.rcgp.org.uk/revalidation-and-cpd.aspx).

Some professional bodies, such as the College of Radiographers and the Chartered Society of Physiotherapists, have an online portfolio which their members can use to chart their professional development. The evidence contained within these portfolios serves to provide proof of CPD for the purposes of registration with the HCPC.

The Institute for Learning (IfL) has introduced the use of e-portfolios to record the statutory 30 hours of CPD now required of the 300,000 practitioners in further education in England.

Although different professions have specific requirements for the recording and evidencing of learning, there are some key aspects that are generally recorded in the portfolio.

> » The experience – what has happened, what has been done, seen, written, read, made, etc.
>
> » The learning – the discovery that what has been recalled has significance for doing or changing things in the future.
>
> » The evidence – a demonstration of how the learning is being applied in an appropriate context.
>
> » Learning needs – an identification of where it would be appropriate to go next.
>
> » Learning opportunities – an educational action plan identifying ways in which learning needs might be met. (Redman, 1994)

The building of the portfolio itself requires engagement in a process of reflection and critical self-awareness. Its creation, therefore, constitutes an educational process in itself. This aspect needs to be recognised over and above the learning outcomes that are identified and evidenced in the physical material contained in the portfolio. In order to make the most use of this educational process, it is likely that the learner may need support during portfolio development. This may be offered through processes such as mentoring, action learning sets, supervision or online support through the portfolio itself or via online forums.

Portfolios within social work

The introduction of the PCF and the change in emphasis in CPD, within both professional standard and regulation contexts, present both a real challenge and a real opportunity for social work. On the one hand, the recent reforms represent the most significant change and commitment towards enhancing social work practice, knowledge and evidence in a generation. On the other hand, the changes represent and require a systemic change in the way that practitioners and employers prioritise and utilise CPD opportunities.

Any change can provoke anxiety, and it does feel like social work is under more scrutiny than ever before. With increasing pressures on public sector budgets and rapid policy changes, both seasoned and newly qualified practitioners can feel isolated and deskilled. Within this context, it can be difficult to find the motivation or direction to create and maintain professional development portfolios. However, it is possible to use a portfolio approach to highlight and maximise learning and reflection opportunities that may have otherwise been overlooked. Formal training is only one of many learning opportunities available, and the following activity will help you to consider how reflection on practice can be used within a portfolio to evidence CPD.

Reflective **activity**

4.3 Using a portfolio for reflecting on practice

Imagine you are trying to show your supervisor that you have approached an event differently as a result of your previous supervision session. Consider how you might use a 'mini-portfolio' to do that.

» Think about what the event is – maybe a court appearance, a difficult discussion with a service user, or a set of notes from a meeting.

» What were you trying to achieve?

» What was different from the last time you did something similar?

» Did your new approach work?

» How do you know?

» What can you use to demonstrate what you have achieved?

Chapter **summary**

This chapter has considered the benefits of using a portfolio approach to learning and development. The changes to social work standards and registration mean that social workers will need to demonstrate on-going CPD and evidence these activities against the standards set out in the PCF.

The HCPC is now responsible for social work registration, and the emphasis is placed on the impact and outcomes of learning activities rather than hours of attendance. While the regulator is set to change in the future, this emphasis is likely to continue and social workers need to be able to conceptualise and link their CPD activities to practise situations as part of their knowledge, skills and capabilities.

Portfolio learning is well evidenced, with examples of effective use across a range of professions and disciplines. The purpose and goal of the portfolio should be clarified from the outset to maximise the learning experience and to ensure appropriate material is provided. Training events are only one form of learning, and development, reflection on practice and collaborative dialogues, along with many other activities, can be used to evidence and achieve your CPD goals and plans.

Chapter 5 | **What goes into a portfolio?**

This book has considered the theory and policy that underpins and guides continuing professional development (CPD) and learning for social work practitioners. Regardless of career level, you will need to think about how your work, training and learning contribute towards meeting professional standards, and you will need to think about developing your own systems and tools for evidencing this and supporting your on-going critical reflection and analysis.

This chapter moves away from the underpinning frameworks and is designed to support you in developing your own portfolio by providing some tools and helping you to think through how you might best structure your portfolio to suit your particular learning needs. This is a practical chapter with suggestions for templates and checklists that can be used to plan your own portfolio. We will guide you through a range of different evidence which you might use to contribute to your portfolio and learning plans. In Chapters 5 and 6, we give you some completed examples of these templates which show what they might look like as you progress through your career.

As registered social workers we all have to evidence CPD activity for our Health & Care Professions Council (HCPC) registration. However, it is likely that you will have other reasons for maintaining your portfolio: evidencing your progress through the Assessed and Supported Year in Employment (ASYE) to show how your practice meets the requirements of the relevant Knowledge and Skills Statements; as part of an accredited programme such as the Practice Educator Programme (PEP) or Approved Mental Health Professional (AMHP); or for appraisal and supervision purposes to keep focused on your own development as a matter of good practice.

Before you start

Portfolios fall into two distinct categories: those for your own personal use; and those which you're putting together to meet someone else's needs or requirements. What you put into your portfolio will depend on why you are developing the portfolio.

Learning how to learn

The first activities in this chapter are designed to help you identify your own needs and preferences as a learner. This will help you when you come to use your portfolio to plan and record your learning activities, and it will make sure that your choices are realistic for you.

You will know from your own experience that people learn in different ways. Even if we attend the same lecture, read the same book or sit in the same meeting, our responses to the situation and what we take away from it vary, and we go away with our own interpretation of what we have been involved in. These differences depend on our own personality and circumstances. The following activity will help you to think about some of the factors that impact on your learning. It will be helpful to do this activity before you start putting together your portfolio, and to return to it on a regular basis as you think about whether your portfolio is meeting your CPD needs.

Reflective **activity**

5.1 Thinking through your own learning

Think of something that you have learned. It doesn't matter what it is – you might think about a skill, a new technique or a new piece of information. When you have identified something, answer the following questions. Note down your answers and retain these for reference.

» What was the learning that you have identified?

» Why did you want to learn this thing?

» Did you find the learning process easy?

» What was it about the experience that you found helped you, or got in the way of your learning?

» How did you or your practice change as a result of this learning?

» What, for you, has been the most significant thing about this learning?

You probably already have some ideas about the sorts of things you like learning, and how you like to learn them. Many people have researched the ways in which people learn, and two names are particularly well known – Lewin (1942) and Kolb (1984). Full details of these authors' best-known works are given in the References, so you can find out more if you want to. In brief, though, both these writers agree that learning takes the form of a 'cycle' that looks something like the one in Figure 5.2.

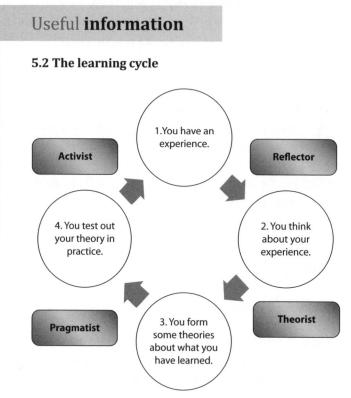

Useful **information**

5.2 The learning cycle

Source: Adapted from Kolb, 1984; Lewin, 1942

You might enter this cycle at any point (in other words your starting point might be an idea rather than a concrete experience), but in order for your learning to become embedded so that you can use it in the future, it is important to go through all of the stages of the cycle.

You will see the words 'Reflector', 'Theorist', 'Pragmatist' and 'Activist' in the different sections of the cycle. These are terms used by Honey and Mumford (1992) to try to identify the characteristics of learning styles at each stage. More details of each style are included in Appendix 3 of this book. Each of the four learning styles identified by Honey and Mumford has its own general characteristics. As you go through the styles, remember that no one will demonstrate the characteristics of only one style, and that these are, to some extent, stereotypical characteristics. They merely indicate preferences and learning habits.

Reflective **activity**

5.3 Applying the learning cycle

Go back to the learning that you identified in the previous activity, or choose another piece of learning, and see if you can identify the stages of the cycle as you went through that learning process.

» What did you do? (Stage 1)

» What did you think when you considered what you had done? (Stage 2)

» What conclusions did you draw as a result? (Stage 3)

» What did you decide to do next? (Stage 4)

» What happened next? (New Stage 1)

We all have strengths and developmental needs, and you will find that there are areas which could be strengthened in order to make you more of an 'all-rounder'. This will make you a more flexible and versatile learner, both academically and professionally. This flexibility will help you when you come to plan, reflect on and record your learning in your portfolio.

Kolb (1984) argues that a mature learner is able to integrate all four styles of learning, and thus will be well prepared to complete the learning cycle. Most people, however, develop learning style preferences that help with some stages, but hinder others. This affects the activities from which they are able to learn the most. It is important that you, as a learner, know what your strengths are, and how you can build on them. At the same time, you can choose to develop those parts of your learning style that are underdeveloped.

Useful **checklist**

5.4 Strengthening your learning

Some strategies that you might use to strengthen your learning styles are provided below. Go through the list and highlight those that you think would interest you. As you go through, try and think of some other strategies you could adopt.

Strengthening 'Activist' style

» Do something you have never done before, and keep trying new things on a regular basis.

» Be more spontaneous; give your view on things.

» Deliberately break up the rhythm of your day, work or study by chopping and changing activities regularly.

» Push yourself into the limelight; make yourself take a more active role.

» Be more positive, enthusiastic and achievement orientated.

Strengthening 'Reflector' style

» Try observing at an event or during a taught session; watch others carefully.

» Let other people speak first; do not feel compelled to respond; listen.

» Use your notes to review a meeting or class; go back over it with a colleague and decide what to do if similar events come up in the future.

» Prepare thoroughly for a future meeting or class; read background material and make notes.

» Research extra well when writing a report or an essay, and make sure you present all points of view before drawing conclusions; go back and review your draft.

» In discussions, make sure you know and understand the views of the other people present; reflect back your understanding to them.

Strengthening 'Theorist' style

» Choose a theory or model for a topic of interest; research it for facts that are for and against; given reasons to explain why the facts do or do not support the theory.

» Look for inconsistencies or weaknesses in other people's arguments, both verbal and written.

» Compare different versions of the same event (eg in newspapers); look for inconsistencies in the facts given.

» Practise using 'what', 'why', 'when' and 'how' questions to get to the heart of a problem; do this in discussion and when reading.

Strengthening 'Pragmatist' style

» When ideas for action occur, write them down then do them as soon as possible.

» In discussions, think about the practical implications of what is being discussed.

» Take every opportunity to go and try something out; use pilot studies.

» Involve others when trying things out; get them to watch you and comment on your progress and technique.

» Think about ways to experiment with theories when they are being discussed.

Your own style of learning is highly individual, and will relate to your personal history as well as your personality, but it will also relate in some way to the cycle described above (see Figure 5.2). The cycle is based on the assumption that, over the years, you have developed learning 'habits' that help you learn more from some experiences than others. Once you can identify these, you will be in a better position to choose learning experiences that suit your own style or, alternatively, to engage in activities that will help you to develop new ways of learning.

Reflective **activity**

5.5 Learning how you learn

Before moving on to the next part of this chapter, write down three events when you learned something new in a way that you enjoyed or found it easy to learn, and three where you found it less enjoyable or difficult to learn.

Alongside the event, write down the type of activity that you had to engage in for your learning to take place. Some examples include the following.

» If you were describing learning to drive, this involves a practical approach to learning, thinking quickly and adapting to new situations, with only a little 'theory' attached.

» If you were describing learning about a famous historical character, you would probably be involved in significant amounts of reading, possibly having to find out where to discover more about this person in the first place, and maybe talking to others to clarify your ideas about what you have read.

You might find it helpful to use a grid like this:

Positive learning experiences	What was involved
1	
2	
3	

Negative learning experiences	What was involved
1	
2	
3	

Then consider the following question.

» Are there any common features among your positive experiences, or among your negative experiences? (Make a note of them, as these will help in your further understanding of your own learning needs and preferences.)

As a result of the exercises you have done in this chapter, you should now be able to outline your strengths as a learner. As a final activity before we move on, identify at least four strengths using the grid below. If you have one or two learning styles that you would like to develop further, write down what actions you will take to help you do this.

Reflective **activity**

5.6 Identifying your strengths

Strengths	Actions to develop learning styles
1	
2	
3	
4	

Throughout this chapter, you have been working through the learning cycle and applying it to your own learning styles. It will now be helpful for you to consider the following questions to check your understanding of your own learning needs using the template provided below, or something similar.

> » What stages of the learning cycle have you experienced while working through this section?

> » Outline each stage and the nature of the activity or experience that you have been involved in. How easy did you find each stage?

> » Does your evaluation of the difficulty of each stage fit in with what you have learned about your preferred learning style, and the areas you have chosen to strengthen?

Reflective **activity**

5.7 Applying the learning cycle

Stage	Activity	Ease of doing for you

Planning your learning

The first section of this chapter was designed to help you to identify your own learning style and the types of situations in which you like to learn. This section will help you to look in more detail at the skills you want to improve in order to make the most of your learning opportunities. In order to do this, it is important that you can identify what your starting point is. Many of the following activities have been adapted from *The Student Skills Guide* by Drew and Bingham (2001). You might want to look at this book for other ideas on improving a range of work and study skills.

It is difficult to think about what you know and can do in an abstract way, such as answering the question 'What are you good at?' It is easier to identify your current skills levels if you think about them in relation to a particular activity, for example, what did completing that essay/attending that meeting/carrying out that task show that you are good at?

As a starting point, think about specific activities that you have been involved in, either on a course, at work or at home, and list them in the grid below.

Reflective **activity**

5.8 Identifying activities

Work activities	Other activities

Now try and break down two or three of these activities into the skills that they involved, for example, negotiating, assertiveness, report writing, gathering and using information, working in a team, time management. Use the grid below.

Reflective **activity**

5.9 Identifying skills

Now try and complete the following skills self-assessment sheet, based on the full list of activities that you identified in the first activity above. Here, you should try to identify not only which skills you need to carry out particular activities, but also to estimate how important these skills are in each context and how good you think you are at each skill.

Activity	Skills used
1	
2	
3	

In the 'Evidence to support my estimate of current skill level' column of the grid below, try to show the evidence to support your estimated skill level. This will give you a guide to where you think there is room for improvement, and begin to help you focus on ways of making that improvement.

Reflective **activity**

5.10 Skills self-assessment

Skill	Activities needing this skill	Estimated level needed (1–4 where 1 = high)	Estimate of my current skill level (1–4 where 1 = high)	Evidence to support my estimate of current skill level
eg Making oral presentations	*Presenting new ideas to my line manager*	*1*	*3*	*I got very nervous last time I had to do one, spoke too fast, and had too much material for the time available*

Now that you have identified skills that are relevant to you, and where there is room for development, you can start to think about how you can make these improvements. Try the following activities as a first step.

Reflective **activity**

5.11 What do you find easy?

What do you find easy or what do you like about the skills you have identified above? Why?

Skill	What I enjoy/like about it	Why?
eg Making oral presentations	*Producing visual aids*	*I am good at sorting out the main points and enjoy making things look good*

Reflective **activity**

5.12 What challenges you?

What do you find difficult/dislike about the skills you have identified? Why?

Skill	What I find difficult/ dislike	Why?
eg Making oral presentations	*I feel nervous about taking questions*	*In case I don't know the answer*

Reflective **activity**

5.13 Doing it differently

Now imagine that those things that you dislike or find difficult are actually things that you are good at. What would you be doing differently? What could you do now to start moving in that direction? It will probably help you to do what you want to if you identify a deadline by which you will have started the process.

Skill	What I'd do differently	How to begin to get there	Deadline to put this in motion
eg Making oral presentations	*Answer questions confidently*	*Try to identify possible questions in advance*	*Next week*

Sometimes, despite all good intentions, you will find that you are not able to meet your deadlines. This might be because you do not have the information or other support that you need to move forward.

Reflective **activity**

5.14 Identifying goals and supports

Make a list in the grid below of the sources of help that you might turn to in order to meet your skills improvement targets. You might want to consider people, places, books or other resources that you could go to.

What I want to achieve	Where I can go for help

In order to achieve any of the above, and fit them in with all the other dimensions of your life at home, work and in studying, you will have to be able to organise yourself and have some time management skills.

Reflective **activity**

5.15 Managing your time

On the chart below, rate yourself on the items given. (A score of 1 indicates that you feel you are very good at this, while a 4 means that you see a need for considerable improvement.) The items listed are just some of the things that will help you to become organised. At the end of our list, you could add some ideas of your own.

	How I score myself (1–4 where 1 = very good)
Being aware of my strengths and weaknesses in how I currently organise my time	
Identifying long-term actions and targets	
Identifying immediate actions and targets	
Estimating how long work will take, and planning ahead	
Reducing things that waste my time	
Meeting deadlines	
Having a well-organised work space	
Having easy to use filing and recording systems	
Other aspects of time management and organisation	

Good planning does not only relate to meeting immediate targets, although these are obviously very important, but you should also have more general targets for where your life is going. What are you aiming for in terms of your learning and your career as a social worker? Within the context of the above long-term aims, you will obviously have short-term aims. These might relate to your work, study or home life. It will be necessary for some of these to be achieved almost immediately in order for you to move on towards your long-term aims.

Reflective **activity**

5.16 Reviewing your goals

What immediate targets do you have, or what things do you have to do now?

How long will each task take? Can these tasks be broken down into smaller 'sub-tasks' to make them more manageable? How does the target fit into your longer-term aims?

Use the following chart to review your immediate targets.

Target/task	Deadlines	Sub-tasks	Deadlines

Now try and answer the following questions to see how your immediate targets relate to your long-term aims.

- » Do my immediate targets support or hinder my long-term aims?

- » Which targets give most support? Which give least support?

- » Do I need to or am I prepared to reconsider or re-prioritise my immediate targets?

- » Are my targets achievable, given the time and resources available?

- » How can I make my targets more achievable? (eg make them smaller or change the time period I have set myself.)

- » What are the conflicting demands on my time that might distract me from my targets?

» Could anyone else take on some of the items on my list of things to be done?

» Do all the things on my list really need to be done?

» What would happen if I did not do one or some of the things on my list?

However well you prioritise what you can foresee, there will be sudden crises that you cannot plan for. This might be sickness, the breakdown of equipment, the unavailability of resources that you had planned to use, or new regulations or policies that you have to work with. You will be able to add to this list, based on your own experiences. The important question for you is: how can you make sure that these unforeseen crises do not throw you off course? There are several possible strategies that you might use. We have listed a few of these below, but you will be able to find others for yourself.

Useful **checklist**

5.17 Helpful hints for managing your time

» Build in time for the unexpected (eg allow for the train to be late, assume there will be a queue at the library checkout, don't leave that phone call until the day you need an answer).

» Add on half as much time again to your estimate of how long the task will take you.

» Delegate some of the work to someone else, and make sure you can 'sell' this by identifying the benefits to them in helping you.

» Share a task with other colleagues or family members.

If time management is one of your development needs, we have included an exercise that you might find helpful in Appendix 4.

All the exercises and activities we have introduced so far are aimed to help you to plan your learning according to your own life, preferred learning style and priorities. Your responses can form the basis of your portfolio. The next set of exercises moves on to focus more on your experiences and how you use them for further learning.

Using your experiences for effective learning

You will have noticed that the notion of reflection keeps recurring throughout these chapters. This is because it is generally accepted by people who understand how learning happens that it is only when you consider your experiences in a structured way that you can use those experiences to influence what you do in future. Schön (1991, 1987) has written extensively about reflection as fundamental to the way in which professionals work, learn and develop, showing how 'reflection on action' (that is, looking back after the event) can help with professional judgement at the time of an event – what he calls 'reflection in action'.

We have included some exercises in Appendix 5 which are designed to help you to use experience, reflection and professional judgement to help you to learn and develop. If you decide to use some of them, you can put them into your portfolio either for your own records or so that you can show colleagues or managers how you are approaching your professional development.

Reflective logs or journals

You may be familiar with a reflective or practice log or journal; these have long been used as part of a portfolio approach to learning. The log could be in the form of a blog or a structured diary. The key to a log, regardless of what format works best for you, is that it provides you with the space to record your thoughts, reflections and plans to support your learning plans and activities. We have included a template for a reflective log in Appendix 5; your log should be kept in your portfolio and will help you to keep track of your learning if you cross-reference it to any certificates, plans or other documents you are storing as evidence.

SWOT analysis

When you come to prepare your personal development plan, you may find it useful to use a SWOT analysis to help you prioritise your learning and actions. SWOT stands for Strengths, Weaknesses, Opportunities and Threats. Using these headings can help you to look at where you are now, and where you might develop in the future, taking into account the range of circumstances that affect how and when you learn. A worksheet to help you work through this model is included in Appendix 5.

'Critical incidents' and reflection

'Critical incidents' can be used as a trigger to help you with your professional reflection. In this context, we are using the term 'critical incident' to mean an event which, for the person who experiences it, has some significance. At one extreme, it may be a turning point in your career, or at the other extreme it may be a routine event which you find yourself questioning, asking: 'Why does that always happen?'; 'What would happen if I did something different?'; 'What's the purpose of doing things like that?' and so on.

There are four stages in working with critical incidents and learning from them.

Firstly, you have to be able to describe the incident itself. Secondly, you move on to look at an explanation or interpretation of the situation you have identified. Your explanation will start off in relation to the specific context but, once you have submitted it to the critical process, you should be able to move on to the third stage and set it in a wider context (philosophical, educational, organisational, etc.). The final, fourth, stage is where you draw conclusions about the significance of the incident, and decide what action you will take as a result of your deliberations.

The four stages of the critical incident analysis closely parallel the four stages of the learning cycle, as shown in the table below.

Useful **information**

5.18 Critical incident process mapped to learning cycle

Critical incident stage	Learning cycle stage
Descriptive or diagnostic	Experience
Reflective	Reflection
Critical	Theorising
Practical	Experimenting

Another way of looking at this way of analysing a critical incident is to take the model of reflection described by Boud and colleagues (Boud et al., 1985, 1993). They offer the following diagram to describe the process (see Figure 5.19).

Useful **information**

5.19 Reflecting on critical incidents

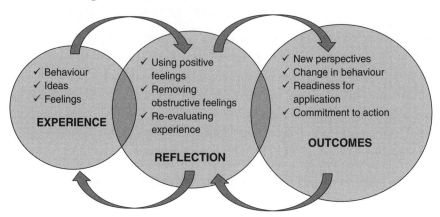

Source: Adapted from Boud et al., 1985, 1993

Reflective **activity**

5.20 Considering critical incidents

Try and work through the process of reflecting on a critical incident for yourself.

Think about something that you have seen or been involved in recently that has made an impact on you. You may choose something that happened at work, at home or during your studies or leisure time. The incident should be something that made you stop and think, that gave you a new insight into what you were doing, or that made you want to find out more about what caused it and what its effects might be.

» Make a note of an incident that you found thought-provoking.

Now go through the following questions, which will guide you through the reflection process and help you to work towards the final stage in the model suggested by Boud et al. (1985). When you get there, you should:

» have new perspectives on and insights into your experience;

» have planned how to change your behaviour as a result;

» be ready to apply your new knowledge;

» be committed to action as a result.

The list of questions is only intended as a guide to your thinking and you will probably explore other areas as well. The 'prompt' questions have been grouped under six headings (see Appendix 5, for the complete set of questions).

» What happened?

» How did you feel?

» How did others react?

» What was good?

» What needed improvement?

» What have you learned?

We have included some additional templates and exercises in Appendix 5 to help you to think about how best to structure your reflections and learning from incidents and experiences. Remember that any exercises that you complete can be used as evidence in your CPD portfolio.

As a social worker, your CPD and learning will need to be mapped across to the capabilities set out in the Professional Capabilities Framework (PCF) and the relevant Knowledge and Skills Statements. Working through the exercises in this chapter and accompanying appendices will help you to reflect on your needs, strengths and professional resources as well as consider specific subjects or skills you wish to develop. As such, the exercises can be used as evidence in several of the capability areas depending on your selected career level. It is helpful if you record which PCF area each activity relates to in your portfolio as this will give you a clear view of any domains that you need to develop or work on to strengthen your evidence.

Chapter **summary**

This chapter has set out a range of tools, information and guidance to help you to think about your own development needs and how these can be recorded and used in your portfolio to help you keep track of your learning and apply a continuous reflective cycle to your practice. All of the tools presented in this chapter and its accompanying appendices can be included in your portfolio as evidence of learning and development, and can be used across a whole range of activities to help you to develop your personal learning plan and your portfolio.

The next chapters of this book will now move on to consider the different stages of your career development and how you can use the tools from this chapter to support you at these different stages.

Chapter 6 | Portfolios in initial education and beyond

As already discussed throughout this book, the overall aim of the Professional Capabilities Framework (PCF) is to provide a common framework for the social work profession to support skill development and to track practitioner learning and development. The process of developing a professional portfolio starts at the point of entry, and this chapter will consider the role of portfolios in qualifying education and how a portfolio can be developed and added to throughout your career.

It is often harder to change when you are used to a particular way of doing things. Therefore, if you are in, or have recently completed, your qualifying course or are embarking on your Assessed and Supported Year in Employment (ASYE), embedding a portfolio approach to your learning in practice at this stage is likely to be of great benefit to the later stages of your career. It will also provide the means to reflect critically on your development pathway as you progress in your professional life.

Social work is a complex and demanding profession, requiring a unique combination of skills and knowledge. Once you qualify, you will be required to be empathetic with service users and colleagues, understand your role in leadership and managing yourself and others, work within a strong ethical framework and understand both the evidence base and the legal frameworks that underpin your actions and decisions. The PCF shows how all these elements fit together and tells you what capabilities you are aiming at during your qualifying course. You will see that there are capabilities that you need to demonstrate before you even enter the course, and these are the things that the university admissions team will be looking for when you go for your interview.

During your course, you will go out on at least two placements – one of 70 days and one of 100 days. These, too, have capabilities attached to them, which link to those you are expected to reach by the time you graduate. The graduation capabilities are closely linked to the Health & Care Professions Council (HCPC) Standards of Proficiency (SoPs) for social workers. You must demonstrate that you are working to these standards before you can register as a social worker, and you must maintain these standards throughout your career in order to remain registered. All approved social work qualifying courses have shown the HCPC that graduates from these courses meet these standards. You will find the SoPs on the HCPC website (www.hpc-uk.org).

This includes details of a consultation to add additional standards to the SoP, including:

» A new standard about social workers being able to identify strategies for professional resilience. The importance of resilience was a theme that came up in a number of activities during the review, including at the workshop we held.

» A new standard about working effectively while holding alternative, competing explanations in mind (4.5). This is intended to augment the existing standard (4.4) about being able to make informed judgements on complex issues, based on the information available.

» A new standard on understanding the principles of information governance and the safe use of health and social care information. This standard was added to the standards for all of the other professions during the last review.

» A new dedicated standard has been created (8.12) about being able to present reports in formal settings.

Your experiences during your course will prepare you for the world of social work, whether you decide to work in the public sector (typically for a local authority), for a charitable or private organisation, or move into practice as an independent social worker once you have gained the appropriate experience. Throughout your course, you will participate in a range of learning experiences including lectures, small group work, independent study, research projects and practice placements. You will also be assessed by a range of different methods: written assignments, research projects, oral presentations and portfolios.

A new approach to social work education

New routes, such as fast-track and career change pathways are developing as the routes into social work professional practice. Both children and mental health graduate programmes, spanning two years and focused on practice-based learning supplemented by focused blocks of teaching, have been developed, with the initial evaluation of the children and families programme Frontline indicating positive outcomes with the initial cohorts of graduates.

Step-up to social work has been developed, again in children and families social work, as a route for more mature entrants who may wish to change career and move into social work practice. As with the fast-track programmes, initial evaluations appear positive and these new routes appear to be providing a real alternative to traditional HEI routes. Regardless of which pathway you might have taken, it is likely that at some point in your training you will have to produce a professional portfolio to demonstrate your learning and that you have achieved the relevant level of capability to progress to the next level.

For more information about Frontline visit www.thefrontline.org.uk.

For more information about Step-up, visit www.gov.uk/guidance/step-up-to-social-work-information-for-applicants.

For more information about Think Ahead, visit http://thinkahead.org.

Portfolios for practice placements

Your practice placements are where you are most likely to be asked to develop a portfolio of your work. The portfolio will probably be assessed by a range of people, for example, your university tutor, your supervisor on the placement, the person charged with overseeing your learning while on placement (usually called a 'practice educator'), and service user and/or carer representatives. The purpose of this portfolio is to demonstrate that you are developing the appropriate capabilities, and that you are able to reflect upon, learn from and link theory and evidence to your practice. It is likely to include a range of evidence sources linked to the PCF and increasingly the KSS, which you will be required to reflect critically upon as part of your evidence.

Useful **information**

6.1 Contents of a placement portfolio

The College of Social Work (TCSW) suggested that, as a minimum, the practice placement portfolio is likely to contain the following.

» Direct observation: at least two for the first placement, and three for the last placement.

» Service user and carer feedback: at least two per placement.

» Critical reflection of practice: at least three per placement.

» Evidence from supervision: an overview record of the supervision sessions that have taken place.

» Evidence from work produced by students for agency: an anonymous summary of the work undertaken during the placement. (TCSW, 2012a)

It is essential that you pass your practice placements. If you do not, you will not be qualified and you will not be able to work in any job which has social work in its title, or undertake certain statutory functions which are reserved for qualified and registered social work practitioners. Consequently, your practice placement portfolio is a key document to enable you to start your social work career.

The portfolio approach is used because it is an ideal way of supporting the development of capabilities and assessing whether they are being attained. It provides a tangible way of showing how you are progressing, which can be used by you and by the people who are supporting your learning. It also helps you and your tutors to understand where your future learning needs lie and how you might address them. Most of all, the portfolio helps you to develop skills of reflection which will enable you to be an effective and professional social worker.

Other portfolios used in qualifying education

The number of portfolios that you will need to produce during your qualifying course will depend on your university and placement providers. However, there are likely to be a number of assessments that require you to take this approach.

Some examples of portfolios that are currently used on some courses are provided below to give you an idea of what you might be asked to produce. You may find that the word 'portfolio' isn't used, but the concept of gathering a range of materials to demonstrate your learning is the same whatever your university calls it.

Accreditation of Prior and Experiential Learning (APEL)

If you already have significant knowledge and experience in an area that is closely linked to social work, it is possible that this can be taken into account when you start your degree. You might be able to enter the course without certain formal qualifications, or it might mean that you can start the course with some credit 'under your belt' without having to re-learn things which you already know and can do. This is called the accreditation, or assessment, of prior learning. In some cases, you may even be able to miss one of your practice placements if you can prove that you can already meet the capabilities at this level of the PCF. This was not allowed under the old regulator, the General Social Care Council (GSCC), but with the transfer of regulatory function to the HCPC, the existing prohibition on APEL for practice will no longer apply.

Any APEL arrangements need to link to the SoPs for social work and the PCF. Higher education institutions (HEIs) should have in place robust and fair arrangements for decisions about APEL in line with the Quality Assurance Agency (QAA) for Higher Education Guidelines on the Accreditation of Prior Learning (QAA, 2008).

Programmes should consider with their partner agencies whether or not they will offer APEL (if they do not, the rationale should be clear) and, if they do, the maximum credits that are acceptable. Assessment of APEL is usually through a portfolio which shows how you meet the learning that you are being credited with.

Transcript of Learning/Higher Education

Achievement Record

All HEIs should have in place a student 'Transcript of Learning' and/or a Personal Development Portfolio, compiled over the programme to communicate information about the students' records (for example, module marks, focus of project work) to prospective employers, either directly or indirectly (through references).

Some HEIs are developing the use of a Higher Education Achievement Record (incorporating the transcript and Personal Development Portfolio). Wherever possible, these processes should ensure that the students' progress in relation to the PCF is recorded. All of these activities are usually presented and assessed through a portfolio-based approach.

The fact that so many different sources of evidence are presented in the practice placement portfolio means that the assessor gains a broad picture of the students' work and supports the students to consider their own practice development in a holistic way. It also helps to ensure that the evidence of learning has been undertaken by the students themselves, as several pieces of evidence are required.

In many forms of independent learning, there is a high risk of plagiarism or reproduction of material that has not been digested or used for learning. Hopefully, you will have a tutor or a mentor who will help you with developing your portfolio and with your reflections on your experiences. This person will not usually be the person who will make the decision about whether your portfolio passes or fails, so you should be able to have an open and honest conversation with them about your hopes and fears in relation to this learning activity.

Practice Educator Standards

Since the closure of TCSW, the status of the Practice Educator Standards have been questioned. It appears that no one organisation owns these and as such while most universities still require an educator qualified to PEP stage 2, there is not a formal requirement for this to be the case. There are a range of programmes and modules that provide the learning required for practice education at stages 1 and 2, but in order to evidence your ongoing capabilities a portfolio should be kept which demonstrates your qualification, ongoing development and currency in practice education practice.

Assessing portfolios in qualifying education

When it comes to assessment, you should be assessed across all nine domains of the PCF. This is known as 'holistic assessment', which means that neither the nine domains nor the capability statements set for each level should be evaluated in isolation from each other.

TCSW (2012e, p 2) offered the following principles and conditions for holistic assessment.

» *Assessment is progressive over a period of time (eg initial qualifying placement, ASYE), leading to effective summative assessment.*

» *Assessment must be consistent with the appropriate PCF level descriptor, and include sufficiency and depth of evidence across all nine domains.*

» *Individual capability statements will be important in terms of providing detail of expectations for each domain, and particularly significant to identify gaps, areas of development or concerns.*

» *The assessment process and judgement must be trustworthy, reliable and transparent (eg include clear guidance in handbooks, assessment panels, triangulated evidence and audit trails).*

» *Evidence must include the ability to reflect critically, including reference to different sources of knowledge and research.*

» *The learner will contribute evidence for assessment but the professional judgement of sufficiency must be made by a registered social worker (at initial qualifying level, assessors must meet the Practice Educator Professional Standards).* (TCSW, 2012e, p 2)

Bearing this guidance in mind will be helpful to students and tutors, supervisors, mentors and assessors when considering the construction and assessment of the portfolio and the purpose which it serves for the students' own learning.

While holistic assessment is the current focus in social work education, it should be noted that other assessment methods are available and in use across other professional groups. The assessment and accreditation system being trialled for post-qualifying children and families social work is a move away from this approach to a more quantifiable and objectively testable methodology.

Currently, the HCPC regulates qualifying courses in social work. However, it is expected that this will transfer to a new regulator over the next few years. Whether assessment and regulation requirements will remain focused on the PCF or move towards assessment against the relevant KSS is currently uncertain.

Assessed and Supported Year in Employment

Once you have graduated and qualified as a social worker, you will be ready to join the professional register and start in your first post. In order to ease the transition from learning in the supported environment of being a student to undertaking a full professional role as a social worker, the Social Work Reform Board (SWRB) recommended the introduction of an Assessed and Supported Year in Employment (ASYE).

The ASYE programme has continued to develop over the last five years and national quality assurance and moderation arrangements have been introduced for those employers accessing funding via Skills for Care. (www.skillsforcare.org.uk/Learning-development/The-ASYE-adults/The-Assessed-and-Supported-Year-in-Employment-Adults.aspx).

During the ASYE, you will have a planned programme of learning which is developed by you and your employer on the basis of a learning agreement which sets out what you want to learn and how your employer will support you in learning it. You should also have a reduced caseload during this period so that you have a real chance to reflect on all the new experiences you are encountering, and to use that reflection for learning. Your aim will be to reach the capabilities set out in the PCF for the end of the ASYE and to meet the requirements of the Knowledge and Skills Statements.

Just as practice placements during qualifying programmes are assessed by portfolio, you will probably find you are asked by your employer to do something similar for your ASYE. By now the concept is probably so familiar to you that you will need little guidance in putting one together. However, now that you are operating as a fully qualified professional, you are likely to find that you are left more to your own devices about what to put in a portfolio.

Useful **information**

6.2 KSS adults requirements for the ASYE portfolio

The KSS for adults set out specific requirements that must be met in the assessment of newly qualified social workers. This provides a helpful framework which you can use to identify the contents of your portfolio for this level of practice. The KSS specifies that the assessment be carried out by a registered social worker and must be based on the following minimum standard of evidence:

» Three (3) formal direct observations of practice carried out by a registered social worker.

» At least three (3) pieces of feedback over the course of the year from people in need of care and support, or their carers.

» At least three (3) pieces of feedback over the course of the year from other professionals.

» The assessment of written work demonstrating the ability to reflect on and learn from practice. It should show how the social worker has used critical reflection to improve skills and demonstrate reasoned judgement.

» The assessment of at least three (3) examples of written reports and records, including a report written for an external decision making process and a set of case recordings.

» The assessor report. (DH, 2015)

Not all social workers will be required to present a portfolio to demonstrate their capabilities. However, a professional portfolio can be just as useful as a lifelong learning tool that will be beneficial alongside any other tests and assessments that are administered in the context of the future assessment, accreditation and regulation systems.

When compiling your portfolio, you should do it in a way that means you are able to see your learning in a holistic way. Whether in electronic or paper form, your portfolio is likely to end up quite lengthy, and mapping activities as you plan or complete them is likely to be a preferable option than trying to do this exercise in retrospect when the learning may not be quite as fresh in your mind.

Whatever system you choose, it will be important to make sure that you are consistent in your approach as you work through your learning programme. This will help you to reflect at each complete stage of development and to see your capabilities across the domains of the PCF rather than in isolation.

Useful **checklist**

6.3 Types of evidence to include

Make sure that within your portfolio you include a range of different types of evidence. These are likely to fall into the following main categories.

» Feedback from direct observations.

» Service user and carer feedback.

» Critical reflection on practice.

» Evidence of learning linked to supervision.

» Feedback from other professionals.

» Evidence from work you have carried out for your employer (eg reports or notes of meetings you have attended or led).

» Other (eg presentations, learning logs, feedback from other professionals, webcam, video recording, live supervision/teaching).

As well as ensuring a broad range of different types of evidence in your portfolio, you might also use more than one example of some types to ensure that you cover all the capabilities and show how your learning has developed. For example, you might want to include notes of a series of supervisions to show how certain topics are progressing, or feedback from service users in different contexts or over a period of time to show how you have adapted to their differing or changing needs.

The ASYE is designed to support your learning and increase your capability by providing a consistent framework of assessment along with the necessary guidance, support and additional learning opportunities to help you grow into a rounded practitioner for whom on-going development planning and evidencing has become second nature.

More information, guidance and a range of templates have been developed by Skills for Care in collaboration with colleagues, as part of a national quality assurance and moderation scheme. These are not mandatory but in order for employers to register and access funding for their newly qualified social workers there needs to be key milestones and quality assurance mechanisms in place. More information about these, including access to key templates, can be downloaded and used in your own portfolios and are also available from most employers providing an ASYE programme. They are available from: www.skillsforcare.org.uk/topics/social-work/social-work.aspx.

Taking your portfolio beyond the ASYE

By the time you have finished your qualifying course and ASYE programme, portfolios will be embedded into your approach to learning. At this point, the challenge becomes how you can take that approach into day-to-day practice. Up until now, you have had structures and requirements placed upon you which you have needed to meet to pass your course, placement or programme. The responsibility for setting the structure and agenda of your on-going development activities and how they are recorded will now pass to you as a capable practitioner in your own right.

While your employer will share some of this responsibility in terms of making sure supervision, CPD and appraisal systems are in place and available, it will be largely up to you how you manage and record your CPD and demonstrate how you meet the standards set out in the PCF.

The HCPC may ask for a CPD profile to support your registration if you are selected for audit (see Chapter 7 for full details). However, this will be an overview and you will need a way of tracking, planning and evidencing your on-going learning for a whole range of reasons and purposes. These might include:

» supervision and appraisal activities;

» when applying for career progression;

» when considering career options;

» when making the case to attend particular events, conferences and courses.

Continuing the portfolio approach you have already become so familiar with is one of the key ways in which you will be able to keep a track of your CPD plans, needs and activities, and continuing the practice is a good way of making sure that you maintain a continuous development record throughout your career.

Chapter **summary**

The way in which initial education and the ASYE scheme are put into practice means that if you are entering the profession now, you are already familiar with and well versed in creating portfolios as part of your learning process. This puts you in a good position as you do not have to make the dramatic changes that more experienced practitioners are now facing.

This chapter has sought to provide an overview of how portfolios are used at the early stages of the career pathway, and there are whole texts dedicated to the subject which provide a much more comprehensive analysis and detailed guidance than we have attempted here. However, it is important to remember that the PCF is a framework for the whole of the social work profession, from entry to strategic leader, and the use of a portfolio, which takes a holistic view across capabilities and encourages reflection, development and on-going learning, is a useful tool regardless of your current career level.

The next chapter moves away from qualification and focuses on how a portfolio can help to guide and shape your CPD plans and activities and contribute to an approach which embeds learning into practice.

All professionals are expected to learn from their own and others' practice, and use this learning to improve their work. This engagement and continuous development is partly what distinguishes a 'profession' from an 'occupation' or a 'job'. This learning is necessary because professionals' work involves them in a series of engagements with service users, projects or concepts, which despite having some characteristics in common, are ultimately distinct experiences. Without a form of structured thought to link these disparate occasions together, the individual does not improve practice, develop professional knowledge or bring about advances across the profession as a whole. This is why throughout this book we have stressed the notion of reflection. Reflection and learning from experience are the essential ingredients of all professional development.

Social workers, like health professionals and teachers, work with vulnerable individuals on a daily basis. They also have to work within bureaucracies and systems which are designed to ensure that there is an evidence base for the professional engagement, and to formalise or routinise the processes and outcomes of that work. Individual social workers are therefore continually balancing what they know with how their knowledge should be used and presented. The more they can ensure that they are maintaining that balance by using or creating evidence, the stronger their professional confidence and identity becomes. However, in order to maintain all facets of the complexities of the job, some external input will be necessary. This is what we generally term 'continuing professional development' (CPD), although Webster-Wright (2009), cited in Brown et al. (2010), prefers the term 'continuing professional learning' (CPL) which, he considers, implies less of a deficit model in exploring where and how learning should be addressed.

This chapter will look at how and why CPD for social workers has changed from an input driven system which counted hours of attendance at courses to a model that puts the professional onus on individuals to identify and find ways to meet their professional development needs. This shift represents a move away from 'doing' CPD to engaging in learning which is based on a range of activities and influences.

Reforming CPD

As we have shown in earlier chapters, social work has been under a spotlight since 2008, with reviews, reports, recommendations and reforms being focused on the profession, all with the aim of improving practice, instilling professionalism and rooting social work within an evidence-based context. In its final report, the Social Work Task Force (SWTF) had strong words to say about the then state of CPD and how it should change in the future, the key theme being that as a profession we should be supporting meaningful CPD as a key factor in quality practice (SWTF, 2009).

In 2009, there was recognition that practitioner development was often not valued either by the person themselves or their employer, and other pressures such as workload and organisational requirements were taking priority to the exclusion of a coherent and consistent approach to CPD. The Task Force also noted that this position was being compounded by a lack of understanding across social work about what the post-qualifying (PQ) framework was or how it should be applied. It was also identified that partnership working across the various stakeholders could improve the position.

Where there are strong partnerships and good collaboration between employers and HEI [higher education institutions] – *for example in commissioning, planning and developing current PQ courses – this has led to a more strategic approach to on-going learning and the exchange of knowledge, more sharing of resources; and positive steps to develop and update practice.* (SWTF, 2009, paragraph 3.4)

Overall, the SWTF review (SWTF, 2009) highlighted that there were significant inconsistencies across social work and no shared understanding of what constitutes meaningful CPD. This was creating a risk in terms of practice development and improvement. The Task Force also highlighted the interactional nature of the profession and recommended engagement with the full range of stakeholders as a key step in resolving the matter.

The Task Force was clear that both social workers and their employers need to take responsibility for enhancing the quality of social work practice, but also that the current way in which CPD was conceived and organised was not sufficient to meet the needs of the profession. It was this view of an inconsistent pattern of CPD that led to the development of the Professional Capabilities Framework (PCF) and a new approach to CPD, under the auspices of the Social Work Reform Board (SWRB) during 2010 to 2012.

Capabilities rather than competencies

The PCF represents a move away from a competence-based approach which risks reducing a complex professional approach to a set of 'tick box' activities which are assessed largely by observation. Instead, the capability approach attempts to define and describe the things that social workers should know and be able to do across the full range of their professional lives. The notion of capability is significant because, as Eraut indicates (1994, p 203), it implies that the individual has the necessary knowledge and skills to perform in a wider range of situations than those that are observed. There is also implicit in this approach an understanding that individuals will understand the role of their profession in relation to individuals, employing organisations and wider society. Capability is about knowledge in use, in context and integrated into practice. None of this can be captured through an atomised approach to practice which defines professionals' performance through a series of tasks and performance-related knowledge.

The SWRB's approach to CPD attempted to capture the idea of capabilities rather than competences by recognising that courses and conferences are not sufficient to ensure that capability is developed and that knowledge continues to be enhanced and integrated into practice.

The responsibility for CPD does not lie solely with the individual social worker. To facilitate a partnership approach to supporting CPD, the SWRB also developed a set of standards for employers and supervision framework. These set out what the employer's role is in facilitating and supporting CPD (SWRB, 2012). The standards state that all employers of social workers should:

» have in place a social work accountability framework informed by knowledge of good social work practice and the experience and expertise of service users, carers and practitioners;

» use effective workforce planning systems to make sure the right number of social workers, with the right level of skills and experience, is available to meet current and future service demands;

» implement transparent systems to manage workload and case allocation to protect service users and practitioners;

» make sure social workers can do their jobs safely and have the practical tools and resources they need to practise effectively. Employers should assess risks and take action to minimise and prevent them;

» ensure social workers have regular and appropriate social work supervision;

» provide opportunities for CPD, as well as access to research and practice guidance;

» ensure social workers can maintain their professional registration;

» establish effective partnerships with HEIs and other organisations to support the delivery of social work education and CPD. (SWRB, 2012)

These reforms to CPD were developed collaboratively, with all stakeholders contributing to the enhancement of social work practice, including people who use services, and carers.

At the same time as the proposals for reform were being developed, the UK government was considering the future of the regulation of the social work profession.

CPD and registration

As discussed in Chapter 1, when the GSCC closed in July 2012 the registration and regulation of social work in England transferred to the HCPC, which has a very different approach to CPD. This change means that social workers now need to think beyond the previous practice of counting their hours, and focus on what difference the CPD activities have made to their practice.

The HCPC standards for CPD span all the professions the HCPC regulates (16 in total), The standards are generic across all professions and social work practitioners will need to be aware of both these and the PCF standards and the relevant KSS when planning their development activities.

CPD needs to be specific to you and your role; it can include a wide range of activities from formal or accredited training, through to using social media, reading and writing or shadowing colleagues. The HCPC will ask for a mix of learning approaches as part of its standards, and this presents you, as a social worker, with an opportunity to be creative in what you use to evidence your on-going development. There are five standards that you will need to evidence. These are shown below for ease of reference.

Useful **information**

7.1 HCPC continuing professional development standards

All registrants must:

1. maintain a continuous, up-to-date and accurate record of their CPD activities;

2. demonstrate that their CPD activities are a mixture of learning activities relevant to current or future practice;

3. seek to ensure that their CPD has contributed to the quality of their practice and service delivery;

4. seek to ensure that their CPD benefits the service user; and

5. upon request, present a written profile (which must be their own work and supported by evidence) explaining how they have met the standards for CPD. (HCPC, 2012a)

As already mentioned in Chapter 1, the HCPC will audit 2.5 per cent of social workers at the end of each two-year registration period to monitor that effective CPD is being undertaken. If you are one of those selected for audit, you will need to provide a written profile, supported by evidence, which explains the CPD you have engaged in and how it meets the HCPC standards. This will include the following.

» **A summary of your practice history for the last two years** (up to 500 words). This should show assessors how your CPD activities are linked to your work. This part of your profile should be used to demonstrate the relevance of your CPD activities and plans to your role and practice.

» **A statement of how you have met HCPC standards of CPD** (up to 1500 words). This statement should show how you and your CPD meet the HCPC CPD standards; you will need to reference all the activities you have taken part in and the evidence you are including. Each of the five statements of standards (see Box 7.1) should be addressed.

» **Evidence to support your statement**. The evidence you send in will back up the statements you make in your CPD profile. It should show that you have undertaken the CPD activities you have referred to, and it should also show how the activities have improved the quality of your work and benefited service users. Your first piece of evidence should include a dated list of all your CPD activities within the audit period. Any gaps of three months or more should be explained. This will help to show the assessors that you meet standard 1. Your evidence should also be able to show that your CPD activities are a mixture of learning activities and are relevant to your work, and therefore meet standard 2.

A template form for your profile is available on the HCPC website (www.hpc-uk.org); however, it is up to you whether you use this or another format for your on-going CPD records.

Your profile will be audited by professionals registered by the HCPC, who have been trained to assess CPD profiles on its behalf.

As we have seen from our description of how adults learn in Chapter 4, this approach to monitoring CPD fits closely with a model of adult learning, and in particular learning from experience. The way in which learning activity is recorded and presented to HCPC is called a 'profile' by HCPC, but is in effect the product of the portfolio-based approach to learning that we have been describing in this book.

How social workers will be regulated in the future, the direction of their CPD activities and how this will be monitored is not yet known. You will need to ensure you keep yourself up to date with the developments as they occur by keeping in touch with the trade press and other information sources.

Aligning the relevant frameworks

The relationship between your own learning, your employment-based appraisal and professional supervision, and your requirements for registration are now clearly aligned. The totality of the reforms across social work qualifying courses and CPD, rooted in the PCF, means that there is now in place an infrastructure that not only enables but facilitates reflective practice for social workers throughout their careers.

The PCF gives the outcomes and capabilities which should be demonstrated at each level and in each domain of practice. The relevant KSS builds on this, specifying the knowledge and skills social workers, practising in particular areas, need to develop and demonstrate.

Mapping your CPD plans and activities to the PCF, KSS and HCPC standards is a useful starting point for the structure of your portfolio as it will help you to keep a focus and provide a framework to help you decide what should and should not be included. As part of a larger portfolio, the HCPC profile can be used as a helpful summary and as a means of monitoring your on-going progress towards your professional and development goals.

The career level you are at will shape the nature of your CPD, and as such your first task should be to identify which PCF level is most appropriate for you given your role, career history and experience. This might be done with your line manager within the context of supervision and appraisal, or it may be ascribed to your particular post by your organisation. For some, this will not be clear-cut and the following activity is designed to help you reflect upon your role and level of capability in order to identify the appropriate career level for you.

Reflective **activity**

7.2 What is your career level?

Your career level is more than what job you happen to be in at the moment, but rather it sets the expectations of your level of capability based on your ability to manage complexity and risk (TCSW, 2012g).

Answer the following questions and then complete the rating chart to help identify the career level that is the most appropriate for you.

» How confident are you of your own practice?

» Is your practice underpinned by reflection and developing understanding?

» What type of judgements do you need to make and how do they affect others?

» How effective are the interventions and skills you use?

» Do you provide leadership or build relationships with others to change practice?

» Are you able to manage complexity and challenge?

» How do you use authority and what authority do you have?

» Do you contribute to others' development, manage services or engage in research activities?

Note down your answers as these can be used within your portfolio as evidence of reflecting on your practice.

After you have reflected on each of these areas, rate yourself on the rating chart below.

Rate each area according to your current practice and role. What is expected of you and how capable are you? Make a note of why you have rated yourself at each level. As a guide:

1 = limited confidence/capability/opportunity;

4 = well-developed confidence/capability/opportunity.

Area	1	2	3	4	Rationale
Confidence					
Autonomy and independence					
Critical reflection					
Professional judgements					
Effective intervention and outcomes					
Working alliances					
Managing complexity					
Managing risk					
Authority and challenge					
Leadership					
Teaching others					

The areas in the chart above are those which you are expected to develop as you progress through the career levels. How you have rated yourself is an indicator of the level you might currently be operating at so, for example, if you rated yourself as:

- » mainly 1s, you are likely to be at social worker level;
- » mainly 2s, you are likely to be at experienced social worker level;
- » mainly 3s, you are likely to be at advanced level;
- » mainly 4s, you are likely to be at strategic level.

If you are a student or an Assessed and Supported Year in Employment (ASYE) practitioner, your career level will already be set, but for others it may not be as clear. Remember that this is only a guide and it can be helpful to talk to your colleagues, managers and service users to see how they would rate your career level.

If you work in children and families or adult social work settings, the relevant KSS will provide additional detail to consider.

The adult KSS states the details of the knowledge and skills expected at the end of the ASYE year and works in conjunction with the PCF domains.

For children and families, three KSS have been set out by the Office of the Chief Social Worker to define the knowledge and skills required of social workers at three different levels of practice; these are:

> » Approved Child & Family Social Worker (ACFSW), for frontline practitioners working within children and families' services. This will be the basis of the assessment and accreditation system (DfE, 2014).

> » Practice supervisor (PS) for those supervising and managing ACFSWs; this will also be subject to testing within the proposed accreditation system (DfE, 2015).

> » Practice leader (PL), for those leading within organisations. The assessment of this level has not yet been finalised but will include specific training, development and support requirements (DfE, 2015).

While these are not formally mapped to the PCF, the two frameworks can be applied together, using the KSSs to define domain 5: Knowledge, domain 6: critical reflection and analysis, domain 7: interventions and skills and domain 8: contexts and organisations, and in the case of the practice supervisor and practice leader domain 9: professional leadership.

Planning, evaluating and reflecting on your CPD

Now that you have a solid and consistent framework within which to consider your CPD, you can begin to put your personal system into practice. Try the following activity to help you think about how you might make a start.

Reflective **activity**

7.3 Planning your CPD

Answer the following questions, note down your answers and store them in your portfolio as evidence of reflection on practice.

> » Think back over the last few weeks or months and try to remember any particular incidents or events that made you stop and think about what

you were doing, or planning to do, and that meant you had to change from your normal practice.

» What was the incident?

» What did the incident require you to change in your practice?

» What did you do about the incident?

» What information did you gather to help you make your decision?

» Where did that information come from?

» What records did you keep during the process?

» What else do you need to do or learn before you can change your practice or put your learning into effect?

» What have you done differently, or what will you do differently, as a result of this reflective process?

» What is the impact on service delivery likely to be?

» How will you recognise or measure that impact?

Now have a look at the PCF and, if appropriate, a KSS (you will find all the details in Appendix 1 and 2) and consider the following questions.

» Which of the nine domains do you think you were working in while you were doing the reflective work described above to change your practice?

» Consider which level you think you are working at: are you newly qualified and undertaking your ASYE, or are you more experienced, possibly a senior strategic manager?

Now look at the description of the capabilities in the domain(s) you have identified at the level you think you are working at (see Appendix 1).

» How far do the capabilities reflect what you actually do in your job?

» Are there some capabilities that you feel confident about and that you can easily demonstrate you're using?

» Are there any capabilities that you think you're a bit weaker on and need to develop? You might want to make a note of these and prioritise them for your next piece of learning.

» What might your next piece of learning look like and where could you find the support you would need to develop that area?

» Could you raise the need for support for your learning in your next supervision session or appraisal event?

Thinking about the relevant KSS:

» Which KSS is relevant to your practice?

» If you work in children and families are you likely to need to progress through the assessment and accreditation system for ACFSW status, or to supervise those who do?

» Do you feel confident that you have the knowledge and skills specified in the relevant statement and are proficient in the roles and tasks identified?

» Are there skills and knowledge you feel you need to develop further or which you have not yet had the opportunity to practise?

» How might you develop those areas?

» What support might you need from your supervisor or manager?

By repeatedly going through this cycle of thinking and doing, you will eventually find your professional practice developing in a measured and relatively systematic way. When linking your personal progress to the organisational context in which you are working, you will find that meeting your personal objectives will also help you to meet your employer's objectives.

CPD and evidence-based practice

Linking thinking and doing is a key part of critical reflection in practice, and social workers should all aspire to taking this type of approach to their CPD as it will support practice improvement throughout their career. The second strand of practice development is evidence-based practice, and you can use a similar approach to that already set out but replace thinking with knowing.

Translating evidence into practice is a key focus of social work education at all levels, and both the PCF and the KSSs, as well as the HCPC Standards of Proficiency (SoPs) for social workers acknowledge that research and evidence should be embedded in practice in order to maximise outcomes for individuals.

Useful **information**

7.4 Recognising the role of evidence in social work CPD

PCF Domain 5: knowledge

Apply knowledge of social sciences, law and social work practice theory

5.10 *Recognise the contribution, and begin to make use, of research to inform practice.*

5.11 *Demonstrate a critical understanding of research methods.* (TCSW, 2012f)

PCF Domain 6: critical reflection and analysis

Apply critical reflection and analysis to inform and provide a rationale for professional decision making

6.6 *Begin to formulate and make explicit, evidence-informed judgments.* (TCSW, 2012f)

KSS Adults

8. Supervision, critical reflection and analysis

Social workers should have a critical understanding of the difference between theory, research, evidence and expertise and the role of professional judgement. They should use practice evidence and research to inform the complex judgements and decisions needed to support, empower and protect their service users.

KSS Children and Families Social Worker

10. The role of supervision and research

Demonstrate a critical understanding of the difference between theory, research, evidence and expertise and the role of professional judgment within that; how to utilise research skills in assessment and analysis; how to identify which methods will be of help for a specific child or family and the limitations of different approaches; and how to make effective use of the best evidence from research to inform the complex judgements and decisions needed to support families and protect children.

KSS Practice Supervisors

1. Promote and govern excellent practice

Interrogate decisions, ensuring they are underpinned by theory and the best evidence and that they will contribute to the goals of the family and their social work plan, whilst ensuring that the safety of children remains the highest priority.

6. Purposeful and effective social work

Ensure methods and tools used are based on the best evidence, that progress is frequently reviewed and that the social work plan is adjusted accordingly.

Practice Leaders

4. Developing excellent practitioners

Critically appraise theory, best evidence and rationale for different practice approaches, and select robust methodologies to form an overarching practice framework. Identify the skills needed to practise within the complexity of children's and families' lives, and in particular the population being served by the organisation.

HCPC Standards of Proficiency for social work

12.3 *Be able to engage in evidence-informed practice, evaluate practice systemically and participate in audit procedures.*

13 *Understand the key concepts of the knowledge base which are relevant to their profession.*

14.5 *Be aware of a range of research methodologies.* (HCPC, 2012b)

14.6 *Recognise the value of research and analysis and be able to evaluate such evidence to inform their own practice.*

The knowing-doing gap

The concept of 'knowing-doing' has been developed within the area of management development and change processes (Angehrn, 2004, 2005a, 2005b) as a result of recognition that there is a gap between what we know and what we do, which is impacted by both a lack of confidence and a lack of motivation to implement change. Many of the principles developed as part of this work can be applied effectively to the process of evidence-based practice and, within the context of a rapidly changing CPD landscape, may help you to think about how you apply knowledge to practice and how this can be recorded within a CPD portfolio.

Angehrn's model sees the link between knowing something and doing something as a linear process, and incorporates the concepts of confidence and motivation as both a help and a hindrance to implementing knowledge into practice.

It suggests that when the professional is in the awareness and interest stages, they are collecting and evaluating information. Within the context of social work CPD, reflection is important at this point as it will help you to work through how the new piece of learning impacts on your practice (see Figure 7.2).

The aim should be to take a critical approach which can then help you to think about how you implement evidence into your practice approach. Once you have developed an understanding, the aim moves towards trying out and adopting the learning in your day-to-day practice capability; at this point you need to consider what motivates you to make the change, and the impact that it will have.

Useful **information**

7.5 The knowing-doing approach

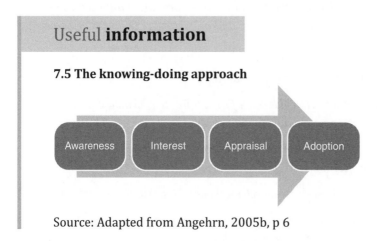

Source: Adapted from Angehrn, 2005b, p 6

This type of reflection is a good example of evidence that can be collected in your portfolio. You may have recorded your thinking in supervision notes, a reflective log or as a written piece. Whichever recording method you use, it can be used to demonstrate your capability in that area and form part of your CPD portfolio.

How can learning be evidenced?

The notion of reflection and the use of a portfolio to plan, record and evaluate learning should now be familiar to you. But what does this mean in relation to demonstrating what you have done and what effect this has had on your practice?

Your work will almost certainly be making you think as well as keeping you busy. However, finding time for structured reflection might be difficult. So, the trick is to make your work and your learning tie together, and use what you do every day to help you with your reflection.

Figure 7.6 shows the type of things that you might be able to use within your portfolio to prompt your learning, record what you have done, and to help you go through the reflection cycle.

You can probably think of other sources of evidence that you can find, or which occur naturally in your everyday practice. Make a note of these so that you can have them to hand while you are thinking about your learning needs and ambitions.

Useful **information**

7.6 Possible evidence sources

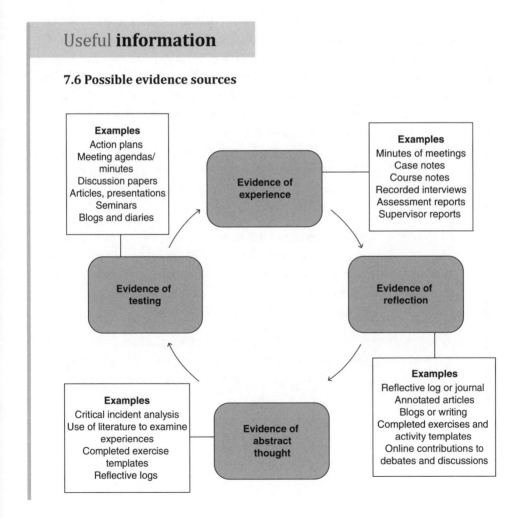

Examples
Action plans
Meeting agendas/minutes
Discussion papers
Articles, presentations
Seminars
Blogs and diaries

Examples
Minutes of meetings
Case notes
Course notes
Recorded interviews
Assessment reports
Supervisor reports

Evidence of experience

Evidence of testing

Evidence of reflection

Examples
Reflective log or journal
Annotated articles
Blogs or writing
Completed exercises and activity templates
Online contributions to debates and discussions

Examples
Critical incident analysis
Use of literature to examine experiences
Completed exercise templates
Reflective logs

Evidence of abstract thought

Chapter **summary**

As soon as you graduate and start work as a social worker, you are already in a position to start thinking about your CPD. The ASYE gives you a gentle introduction to learning from your work and considering future learning needs. The capabilities in the PCF at ASYE level and the KSS give you and your employer a framework for learning and assessment. This will help you to understand your job and what is required of you, and how to reach the level of performance that is expected by the end of your first year in practice. Your employer will probably provide you with a structured learning programme, which means that you should be able to get the help and support you need to provide the bedrock of your future approach to CPD.

One further point on CPD: it is not a solitary activity. As you engage with others and learn from and with them, you can expand your horizons beyond what you could achieve on your own. Your portfolio can have a role here too. You can choose how much or how little of your portfolio you share with others. You can also choose how far your portfolio is developed as part of a collaborative process. If your portfolio is in an electronic format, by working with others on what you put into your portfolio, this can become a place where you blog, discuss, share and create knowledge instead of your portfolio being merely a 'filing cabinet'. That is your choice and is an advantage of an electronic approach to portfolio building that has not been available to previous generations.

As you go through your career, you will have a choice of development routes. The PCF offers capability statements for several of these. For example, you can become a consultant social worker or professional educator, maintaining your front line work and supporting others, or follow the management route where you take a more strategic approach to social work services.

As you consider your work, reflect on it and plan your next steps, your portfolio will provide a record for you to look back on how you came to make your career choices, and which strengths and preferences you were building on.

Chapter 8 | Portfolios for career development

This book has so far considered the use of portfolios from a learning and development perspective, and as a means of storing, evidencing and reflecting on development to improve practice.

In addition to being a learning tool, a social work professional portfolio can also be used to assist in career planning, and this chapter will consider career aspirations and link these to portfolio activities in order to assist reflection and evaluation of future plans and practice development.

Prior to 2009, there was the lack of a consistent and clear career pathway which enabled social workers to remain in practice and develop advanced skills, with practitioners moving into management and education roles to enhance their careers. This issue was highlighted as a concern by the Social Work Task Force (SWTF), and a framework was developed by the Social Work Reform Board (SWRB) which embedded the concept of a career pathway within the Professional Capabilities Framework (PCF) and provided routes of progression that were linked to particular capabilities.

In Chapter 7, we considered what career level of the PCF you were at in terms of the capabilities which were relevant to your continuing professional development (CPD) plans and evidence. One of the benefits of a clear career pathway is that it makes planning for career development a much easier task as you are able to follow a defined pathway in terms of what is expected, and in this chapter we will be thinking about how a portfolio could be used to support your career development through the PCF pathways.

Social work career pathways

The key contribution of the career pathways set out by the PCF is that there are three possible pathways for career progression which recognise the contributions of practitioners, educators and managers within the context of the profession. This means that direct practice now offers more opportunities for development than was previously the case, and there is now more recognition that, along with management and educational roles, the capabilities of front line practice are valuable and should be defended and guarded.

While some may aspire to the routes of progression which management and academia may offer, there are also practitioners who, given the opportunity, would choose to remain in practice and develop more advanced skills and seek to lead from the front in terms of embedding and modelling an ethos of quality into front line and organisational social work practice. The route that is more appropriate to your career aspirations will determine the capabilities you will develop. All three routes start with developing experience as a social worker, and it is only at advanced level that different pathways, accompanied by the appropriate capabilities, come into play.

Useful information

8.1 PCF career pathways

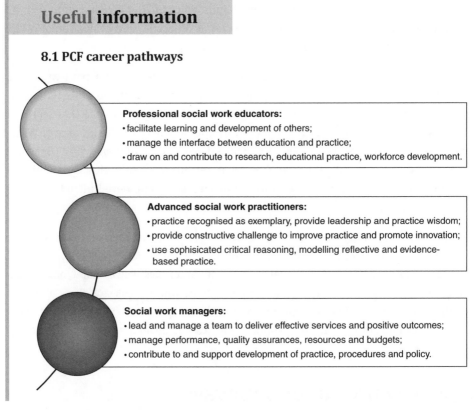

Professional social work educators:
- facilitate learning and development of others;
- manage the interface between education and practice;
- draw on and contribute to research, educational practice, workforce development.

Advanced social work practitioners:
- practice recognised as exemplary, provide leadership and practice wisdom;
- provide constructive challenge to improve practice and promote innovation;
- use sophisicated critical reasoning, modelling reflective and evidence-based practice.

Social work managers:
- lead and manage a team to deliver effective services and positive outcomes;
- manage performance, quality assurances, resources and budgets;
- contribute to and support development of practice, procedures and policy.

The final level of the framework is the strategic level, where roles such as the principal social worker (PSW) are located, creating a coherent pathway for practice, education/academia and management for social workers to progress.

The benefit of a framework such as the PCF is that you are able to plan your development activities to help you achieve your career goals as the expectations of each level is clearly defined. Figure 8.1 provides some more detail of the three pathways to help you consider which pathway is likely to be most appropriate to help you achieve your career aspirations (TCSW, 2012d).

Career levels

The PCF sets out six career levels which are designed to support practitioners to build upon their professional capabilities and learning throughout their career. The exercise in Chapter 7 (see Activity 7.2) is designed to help you to identify your career level and help you to think about what that means for your own development and how a portfolio could be used to track your progress through the career levels on your preferred pathway.

Full details of the various levels can be viewed and downloaded from BASW's website (www.basw.co.uk/resource/?id=1137), but in brief are as follows.

Student level

From the point of entry, social work is now seen as a pathway through which practitioners develop and refine their skills, knowledge and capability. Chapter 5 considers briefly how a portfolio approach is currently used at this level.

ASYE level

The first year in practice is now seen as developmental and offers an opportunity to assess capabilities and provide targeted support. Chapter 5 briefly considers the role of portfolios at this career level. These capabilities build upon those set out and developed in the previous level.

Social worker level

This level sets out what is expected in capability terms from a front line level social worker, how you monitor and record your CPD activity, and the impact it is having becomes your responsibility. The structure of a portfolio can help you to develop your practice capabilities as you take on increasing responsibility as an independent practitioner. Chapters 6 and 7 provide some thoughts and suggestions about how a portfolio can be used for the purposes of on-going CPD.

Experienced level

As practitioners become more experienced and confident in their practice and decision making, they are likely to take on a more supervisory role, informing and directing the practice of others through supervisory relationships or taking on statutory duties such as becoming an Approved Mental Health Professional (AMHP) or Best

Interest Assessor (BIA). Chapters 6 and 7 provide some guidance on portfolios for CPD and these can be used to evidence competence in various roles as well as providing evidence of capability development.

Advanced level

At the more advanced level, practice and professional leadership is a key focus, and your development activities and needs may become more specialist and diverse. At this point in the career framework the three pathways are introduced, namely education, practice and management. This level of the PCF has a number of core capabilities that are common to each pathway, and supplementary capabilities that are expected based on the chosen pathway. As with previous career levels, taking a portfolio approach will assist you to take a holistic view of your development activities and outcomes, and to identify any gaps in your capabilities that need to be addressed to enable you to continue to progress.

Strategic level

At this final level of the PCF, social workers will be expected to work at a strategic level within the profession or organisation, with influence and impact on organisational awareness of and response to the views of people who use social work services, communities and the political context within which they are operating. The role may be varied and require a wide range of evidence to demonstrate credibility and on-going capability, for which a portfolio-based approach may be beneficial.

Progression between levels

As the PCF is a career framework rather than an occupational framework, the levels and pathways set out will not always be clearly associated with the roles and job functions that are in existence across the sector. Therefore, whether you know which pathway you are following or whether your organisation has acknowledged your current career level, it will be useful to consider how you evidence and reflect on a number of key areas as you will need to be able to demonstrate greater capability as you progress. Career progression through the levels should be characterised by:

development of people's ability to manage complexity, risk, ambiguity and increasingly autonomous decision making across a range of situations. (TCSW, 2012c, p 1)

For children and families social workers, achievement of the ACFSW status, or recognition at practice supervisor or practice leader levels of the KSS will be significant milestones.

It can be difficult to evidence the development of particular skills, especially those which are interpretive and subjective. A portfolio approach will help you to demonstrate progress over time by collecting and reflecting on practice on an on-going basis, using your day-to-day practice as an evidence source from which clear evidence of capability development can be drawn.

At periodic intervals, it is useful to evaluate your progress towards your overall goal. The following activity questions will help you to consider your progress from a more critical perspective. This activity can be used either as an individual reflection or as part of your supervision or appraisal as a way of carrying out a quick stocktake of where you are in relation to your career goals. You should record your responses within your portfolio as they will provide evidence in relation to several domains, including domain 1 professionalism and domain 6 critical reflection and analysis, which you can use to show your developing capability.

Reflective activity

8.2 Periodic review and identifying progression

As part of your on-going CPD plan, set yourself regular review points and reflect on how you are progressing. The following questions are designed to help.

» Have you completed your development goals according to your plan?

» If not, why not? If so, what have you found helpful/a hindrance to achieving your goals at this point?

» What are your key learning points from your development opportunities since you last reviewed your progress?

» What were the expected learning goals you had planned to achieve?

» Have you achieved these goals?

» What plans do you have between now and your next review?

» What do you need to change/improve/maintain over the next period?

» What difference have your development activities made to your career development plans so far?

Remember to note down your answers and keep them in your portfolio.

How can a portfolio help with career development?

CPD used to be something of an afterthought in a pressurised environment, and you may find that as you climb the ladder your CPD and critical reflection activities become more ad hoc and opportunistic rather than part of a coherent plan. For social workers operating within multi-disciplinary or management-orientated environments, the concept of supervision is likely to be more closely associated with performance than it is with development.

As a framework, the PCF provides a great deal of clarity in terms of what standards are expected as you become more experienced and take on more responsibility and accountability.

The Local Government Association (LGA) has also developed some standards for employers of social workers in England to help them to create an appropriate environment for good social work to be carried out (www.local.gov.uk/workforce/-/journal_content/56/10180/3511605/ARTICLE).

These standards, combined with the PCF, should help you to plan your career development in a more coherent way and link it to the achievement of specific skills and capabilities.

By mapping your capabilities against the nine domains of the PCF at your particular career level, or if you are focusing on progression at the career level you are aiming to achieve, you will be able to plan and undertake CPD that helps you to develop in a particular way and that helps you to work towards your particular goals and aspirations. You will find some exercises and templates throughout this chapter, and in the appendices of this book, to help you to identify your own strengths and needs for career development.

Regardless of your current career level, there is always more to learn, and continuing to maintain a professional portfolio from the earliest possible stage is likely to provide you with a sense of direction that would otherwise not be so apparent.

As practitioners in an evidence-based profession, social workers need to make sure that their practice is based on the best available information and as such, regardless of which pathway you prefer, you will need to apply a critical reflection perspective to your own capabilities and development activities.

Critical reflection is an approach defined as both an individual domain and as a common theme throughout both the PCF and the KSSs. It is seen as a fundamental element of professional practice and the linchpin of sound professional judgement and decision making (DfE, 2014; DfE, 2015; DH, 2015; SWTF, 2009; Munro and Great Britain Department for Education, 2011; SWRB, 2012; TCSW, 2012c, TCSW, 2012d).

Critical reflection has significant evidence supporting its usefulness for the development and quality assurance of social work practice (Fook and Askeland, 2007; Askeland and Fook, 2009; Fook and Gardner, 2012; Gardner and Fook, 2012) and should be applied to all development activities whether the focus is on developing capabilities or progressing through your preferred career pathway. Recognising your own needs and knowledge gaps is a key part of career progression and serves two purposes. Firstly, it demonstrates accountability and integrity in your approach as you are being honest about the limitations of your capabilities. Secondly, it provides a focus for your CPD planning as it identifies which capabilities need further development if you are to achieve your career goals. For this to be the case, you will need to think about and identify your career aspirations once you achieve the level of experienced social worker.

At this point, you will have the option to follow three distinct pathways, and the development activities and evidence needed for each of these will differ. As a first step, it will be important for you to reflect on any gaps in capability that need to be developed as part of your CPD plan in order to support your progression through your preferred pathway.

Practice example

8.3 Identifying gaps for CPD planning and career development

It is likely that you have areas of both strength and development needs within the PCF domains or KSS elements, and it is helpful to map your capabilities to help you identify the areas to target in your CPD plans.

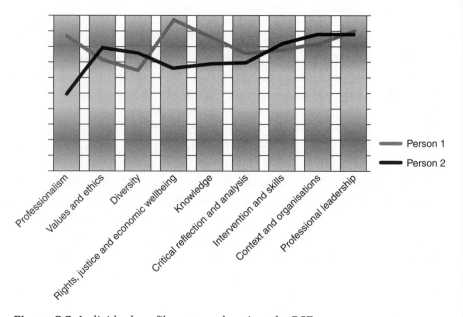

Figure 8.2 Individual profiles mapped against the PCF

Figure 8.2 shows two social workers at the same career level who have mapped their capabilities across the nine domains. This is a self-assessed activity which you should record in your portfolio as it evidences your ability to reflect on your own practice skills.

Person 1: This profile suggests that the individual sees themselves as particularly strong in terms of the rights and justice elements of the PCF, but that they have identified that the domain of diversity is an area for development. This may be someone who has noticed that their local population is changing and is concerned about how this impacts on their services and practice. In this context, you would expect the person's CPD plans and learning to include activities and reflective work in relation to this domain to support capability development.

This might include, for example, considering case work in supervision from a diversity perspective and reflecting on the impact of this on their practice within their portfolio; researching local population trends and reflecting on what this might mean for their practice.

Person 2: This profile suggests that the individual sees professionalism, that is, acting within the role of a professional social worker, as the capability they most need to develop. This may be someone who has only recently moved into a social work role or who has moved into an unfamiliar area which has changed how they see themselves and their role as a professional social worker. In this case, you would expect that this would be the area that features in their CPD plans and activities.

This might include, for example, shadowing colleagues in particular roles and tasks that are associated with social workers, and reflecting on the skills and capabilities demonstrated, and undertaking a critical analysis of a social work task to break down the various steps.

The same exercise can be carried out with the KSS. For example, a profile against the child and family social work KSS might look like the following illustration.

As with the PCF illustration, it is likely that different practitioners have strengths and development needs in different areas and this can inform the focus of professional development planning.

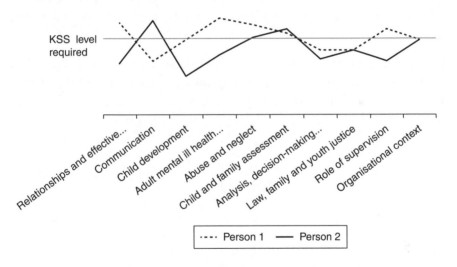

Once you have identified your current career or KSS level, your career goals and your capability gaps, you will have a clearer idea of what you need to achieve in order to reach your professional aspirations.

The range of tools and activities set out throughout this book and its accompanying appendices may help you to work through and structure your reflective processes. One of the most common sources of evidence is a reflective practice log or journal, and this type of approach should also be used in your career planning to help you keep a critical view on your progress and achievements, and to allow you to adapt your plans where activities are becoming less targeted towards achieving your goals and aspirations.

It should be noted that the development of capability on its own will not guarantee you the job of your dreams. Both the PCF and the KSS and your portfolio are career tools and are not job role specific. When you apply for jobs, you will still need to put together a good written application, interview well and demonstrate that you are the best person for the job.

Chapter **summary**

The concept of career levels and pathways with specific expectations and standards are embedded in the PCF, and social work CPD should consider the building of capabilities specific to the preferred pathway.

The portfolio approach described and explored in Chapters 6 and 7 in relation to evidencing capability and on-going learning is also effective for demonstrating career progression and helping you to develop a more in-depth understanding of social work evidence-based practice in your chosen area.

While a good portfolio will not guarantee you a job, it will ensure that you develop and are able to evidence the capabilities expected by both the profession as a whole and its employers at the more senior levels.

Chapter 9 | **How are portfolios assessed?**

This final chapter considers some of the various ways in which a portfolio can be assessed to help you to make the best use of your portfolio for learning purposes.

Once a portfolio has been developed, it has to be used for something or it has no value or purpose. One way to judge the value and purpose is to submit it for assessment.

Assessment

Assessment might be undertaken formally by an independent person who has not had any involvement in the portfolio, or by someone who has a role in supporting the learner in putting the portfolio together, or by the learner themselves.

The assessment may be either formative – designed to aid learning and give feedback to the learner – or summative – with a purpose of marking an end point of a learning episode and possibly certificating or making an award based on the outcome of the assessment.

Teachers, tutors, supervisors and managers all engage in both formative and summative assessment of learning, although the terminology may differ depending on the context. For example, professional supervision and appraisals are just as much forms of work-based formative assessment as giving feedback on an assignment during a degree programme. The outcome of a promotion interview involves the application of summative assessment skills which are equivalent to those used by a member of academic staff marking a Master's degree dissertation.

Portfolios offer the same potential for formal and informal, formative and summative assessment as any other learning and support activity. Their use across all levels of initial and continuing professional education as a tool in evaluating progress is well established and documented (Usherwood et al., 1994; Snadden and Thomas, 1996; Challis et al., 1997; Challis, 1999). However, portfolios' use in summative assessment took longer to be accepted, largely because of concerns over reliability and 'trustworthiness' of assessment. Nonetheless, within higher education and continuing professional development (CPD), there is now acceptance that the portfolio can be used for summative assessment – that is, to demonstrate that the learner has achieved some predetermined outcomes which mark the end point of that learning episode. Indeed, doctors in general practice are required to keep an e-portfolio and submit it for assessment in order to gain revalidation so they can remain in practice in the UK.

Much of the movement towards the acceptance of portfolios for 'high stakes' assessment may have arisen from the development of structures for the accreditation of prior experiential learning – largely prompted by the introduction of National Vocational Qualifications (NVQs) – and the development of work-based learning routes into and through higher education (Brennan and Little, 1996). These two major fields of work in the worlds of academia and CPD have demonstrated that summative assessment using a portfolio of evidence of learning may be undertaken with the degree of reliability normally expected within higher education.

Who will assess your portfolio?

Assessment may be undertaken by individuals reviewing and developing their learning (self-assessment). Alternatively, it may be done by another person who is in a position to make a judgement about the processes and outcomes of the learning.

Employer endorsement processes

Employer endorsement is the first stage of the assessment and accreditation scheme. It is the opportunity for employers of child and family social workers to apply a robust assessment of individual practitioners and to determine the baseline quality of a social worker's knowledge and skills.

Employers will wish to assure themselves that any social workers they put forward for assessment, at either ACFSW or PS levels, are equipped with the skills and knowledge required and that those undertaking supervision of those practitioners meet the standards expected of this role and are competent, confident and capable of supporting others to achieve best practice standards.

Guidance is in development at the time of writing, with implementation and publication scheduled for June 2016. The guidance is intended to provide employers with options rather than being prescriptive, and social workers will need to familiarise themselves with their employers' systems and processes and tailor their professional portfolios accordingly. More information and access to the guidance will be available from June 2016 at http://daisyboggconsultancy.co.uk/employer-endorsement.

Assessing e-portfolios

Both electronic and paper-based portfolios can be assessed, and both formats offer similar learning benefits to the people constructing them. The Joint Information

Systems Committee (JISC) has carried out research into the use of e-portfolios both in higher education and in professional practice. Their 2012 publication, *Crossing the Threshold: Moving e-Portfolios into the Mainstream* (JISC, 2012), offers a toolkit on implementing an e-portfolio and a range of key messages from practitioners who have managed the process of making e-portfolios a normal part of their practice.

The publication, *Effective Practice with e-Portfolios* (JISC, 2008), focuses on the role that e-portfolios play in the formative processes of learning, for example, by supporting dialogue with peers and tutors, evaluating and celebrating personal achievements and skills development and, in the process, engaging learners and professionals in more profound reflection on their personal development planning and CPD.

The JISC research indicates that e-portfolios lend themselves to assessment in the same way as more traditional paper-based portfolios. An e-portfolio, like its paper equivalent, is produced at key points in a learning journey, for example, when demonstrating the outcomes of learning, applying for a job or the next stage of learning, or seeking registration with a professional body. Like their more traditional counterparts, e-portfolios demonstrate what is important about individuals at particular points in time – their achievements, reflections on learning and a picture of their abilities, aspirations and ambitions.

An e-portfolio system or combination of tools that supports reflection, collaborative activity and the preparation and presentation of evidence of achievement provides crucial opportunities for personal development. The accumulated store of reflections, experiences and achievements – which might include aspects of informal, unstructured learning as well as that resulting from engagement in formal education – may be presented as evidence for formal assessment. But it may also be retained as a personal document, as an evolving story of an individual's learning journey. E-portfolio content developed purely for personal reflection and not shared with others can still support formal and more public forms of learning. In this way, e-portfolio development may be seen as the centre of learning rather than as a peripheral activity or by-product of learning.

Rigorous assessment of portfolios

In order to maintain the rigour of portfolio-based assessment, we suggest that the assessment process should be framed by the following guidelines.

> » Assessment is carried out within a criterion-referenced rather than a norm-referenced system. This means that each portfolio is seen and assessed on its own merits, and is not compared with other portfolios or

learners' achievements. 'Grading' portfolios, while not impossible, may require a rigidity of format that is counter-productive to the learner-centred philosophy underpinning the use of portfolios.

» The criteria for assessment – that is, what the assessor will be looking for when reviewing the portfolio – should be explicit and known to (or, if appropriate, negotiated between) both learner and assessor.

» The portfolio should be based on specific learning outcomes or objectives which form the personal learning plan or personal development plan. These objectives should be written in such a way that the evidence of achievement can be assessed. For example, an outcome such as 'understand the principles of ...' is not readily assessable because 'understanding' is an indefinite term open to many levels of interpretation. Objectives which use words such as 'explain', 'evaluate', 'analyse' and 'illustrate' enable both learner and assessor to approach the evidence of learning from a common standpoint.

» The evidence of learning selected by the learner for assessment is supported by a verbal or written reflective explanation of why each piece of evidence has been included, and the part it has played in the progression of the learner's thought and practice in achieving the learning objectives.

» It should be ascertainable that the evidence is by or about the learner (authentic), that it is an appropriate indication of the learning claimed (valid) and applied, and the assessor should be able to infer that the learning is still current.

What does a good portfolio assessment scheme look like?

Baume (2001) has outlined what he believes to be the features of a good portfolio assessment scheme. These are summarised below.

Validity

A good, valid assessment scheme tests whether the learner has achieved the goals set out when devising the portfolio. These goals may be expressed as the intended learning outcomes of a course, or in terms of knowledge to be learned or professional or academic values to be demonstrated.

Reliability

Under a good assessment scheme, the assessment criteria are so well specified and the assessors briefed, trained and in such close agreement over the meaning and application of these criteria that different assessors agree closely on their assessment judgements on a given piece of work. That is, the assessment scheme is reliable.

Fairness

Fairness is a subjective concept. Validity and reliability contribute to perceived fairness, and so, often, does the principle that equal marks should reward equal effort. It is difficult to accommodate fairness into our assessment practice, but we can specify maximum portfolio size as a partial and reasonable proxy. Portfolios can be described and perceived as fair in that they allow learners to present their own selection and their own analysis of their own work, undertaken over a period of time and with access to information and other resources.

Value

A good assessment process allows learners to produce work that they value and in which they take personal and professional pride. Because a portfolio is derived from and demonstrates the learner's own experiences and learning, it is more likely to be valued by its producer than a single essay or exam script. The reflection on the portfolio makes it part of the professional and personal development of that individual – almost an extension of their own life.

Efficiency

A good assessment process makes efficient use of both the student's and the assessor's time and effort. However, the potential scale and complexity of portfolios means that their development and assessment may be very time consuming for both the learner and the assessor. Despite the amount of time and effort for the learner in planning, producing evidence and reflecting on learning, these activities are of educational and developmental benefit, even without the results that may accrue from assessment.

There are ways in which the efforts of the assessor can be manageable and realistic. For example, it may be possible to put an upper size limit on the portfolio to make the sheer volume less. Focusing on the reflective accounts, verifying that the evidence is what it claims to be, and using the evidence to support these accounts means that the assessor may be able to form a confident judgement without having to scrutinise every piece of evidence in detail.

Openness

A good assessment system has no secrets. Learners and assessors know and understand the planned outcomes, the assessment criteria and the assessment process.

Self-assessment for planning, progression and registration

Self-assessment takes place when you compare your performance – as identified in your portfolio – against some concept of ideal or desired practice. The Professional Capabilities Framework (PCF) and the KSS give you those benchmarks so that you can constantly check that you are not falling behind that level of performance.

In reflecting on your practice, you should identify those things that prevent you doing as well as you want to, or stand in the way of your learning and putting new information and skills into practice.

It will be impossible for you to make advances in all domains of the PCF or the KSS in a single week, month or even year. However, you might be able to take a single element of your practice and consider how you can improve it, using your portfolio to chart your progress and to give you the material to support your reflection.

The PCF gives a breakdown of what professional practice should look like at different career levels for social workers. The Health & Care Professions Council (HCPC) has set minimum standards of proficiency for social work. If you fall below these standards, you will not be able to register with the Council, and will be unable to practise in social work roles. Your portfolio can help you to make sure that you meet the HCPC threshold standards as well as continuing to progress professionally through your career. The future of registration is currently under review and a new regulator will produce its own requirements for demonstrating CPD.

Practice **example**

9.1 Reflecting on specific skills

Let's consider communication skills. You will probably find that your practice varies from day to day, depending on a range of things including your own mood, the people you are communicating with, and the means you are using for the communication (for example, written, oral, individuals, groups).

Consequently, your pattern of effectiveness in communication may be a zig-zag shape, moving up and down from the baseline level required for professional practice. When you feel you have hit 'rock bottom' – that is, the minimum professional requirement – you may find that you have an 'Aha' moment: a moment of clarity about what it is that brought you to this low point.

This gives you the possibility of considering how to avoid reaching this point again and of choosing the learning route, or change in practice, that will keep you above the minimum threshold level of performance.

Figure 9.1 illustrates this process.

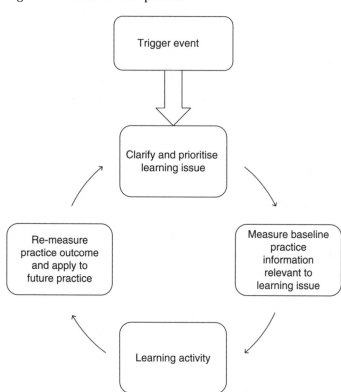

Figure 9.1 Reflecting on practice

Your portfolio will help you to engage in this continuous cycle of recording, reflecting, learning and taking action. In order to make sure the portfolio is up to date and contains everything you want to keep in it, you might like to give yourself a regular time to review your portfolio – maybe once a month. You can use this time to check contents and to use your overview of what is in there to undertake your reflections and write them down. In this way, you can set your starting point for the next circuit of your learning cycle and watch how your learning and practice evolve over time.

Formative assessment for progression, appraisal and supervision

Formative assessment is a process where someone else gives you feedback on what you are doing or planning to do to help you to improve. A portfolio can form the basis on which this feedback is given. It may be used by tutors and educators supporting the social worker's learning in the context of an educational activity, or by managers or colleagues who are offering support and development opportunities through mentoring, professional supervision or appraisal.

Due to the fact that different people learn things in different ways, it is not enough only to look at the outcome of learning and judge whether particular outcomes have been achieved. What we are talking about with formative assessment is making judgements about the journey that the learner is taking.

Useful **checklist**

9.2 Effectiveness of learning cycles

If you are in a position where you are being asked to give formative, developmental assessment, you may want to try to evaluate, with the learner, the effectiveness of the learning cycles described above and in Figure 8.1. In order to do this, you might want to think about the following.

» Has the learning need arisen as the result of a systematic process of identifying where and when the learning is needed? This means that the social worker has looked carefully at his or her practice and decided from this which areas need to be concentrated on.

» Has the identified need resulted in a learning activity that is likely to have significant impact either on outcomes for service users or on the social worker's practice?

» Does the learning need clearly relate to the professional needs of the social worker – has it been identified from a critical incident or similar occasion as the 'trigger' for learning action?

The outcome of a learning cycle should meet or exceed the pre-established standards or capabilities identified at the beginning of the cycle. These may derive from the PCF, the KSS or the HCPC Standards of Proficiency (SoPs), or from some other targets set by tutors, supervisors or managers.

The outcome should be measurable using either quantitative methods (ie using numbers or statistics) or qualitative measures (eg using perceptions, feedback or critical reflection).

Each completed learning cycle should be accompanied by conclusions and/or action points as well as reflection on the learning.

Summative assessment of achievement

Summative assessment is used when learning has reached some form of end point, such as the completion of a phase of qualifying education or a practice placement, or the end of a period of registration. It is considered to be a 'high stakes' assessment as it may influence the future career of the social worker. The role of the portfolio during summative assessment will be to ensure that the link between learning and practice is made, and that this is viewed within the context of the target outcomes which have driven the learning.

Effective summative assessment will influence learning. We know that learning that will be assessed is undertaken using two broad approaches: surface or deep learning (Marton and Saljo, 1984). Surface approaches are characterised by the rote learning of facts and their reproduction (frequently under formal examination conditions). Deep approaches involve individuals attempting to understand underlying principles, ideas and concepts and interpreting these in personally meaningful ways. These approaches are not mutually exclusive. What determines whether a learner adopts a surface or deep approach is primarily a mix of prior educational experience and the nature or structure of the particular task in hand.

Tutors in universities are trained and experienced in summative assessment. University qualifications depend on assessment that meets the requirements relating to quality and standards both within their institution and across the whole of higher education. In relation to social work education, the HCPC will also want to know that assessment is carried out consistently by appropriately qualified and competent people. The Social Work Reform Board (SWRB) has made recommendations relating to the qualifications of practice educators, which should ensure that a rigorous and reliable approach to both formative and summative assessment is embedded within practice placements.

Giving supportive feedback

Whatever the purpose of the portfolio, and whether assessment is for summative or formative purposes, a key to success will be how the learning is evaluated, considered and used for further development. A component part of this is how feedback is given and received. This feedback may be verbal or written, and may be part of formal assessment or appraisal or be offered as informal reflections from a mentor or colleague. The feedback should always be constructive, with the purpose of making a difference in the behaviours or skills of the receiver.

Much has been written about the range of techniques for giving and receiving feedback, and many of the skills needed are part of the social worker's everyday tools in working with service users and colleagues.

Effective feedback relies on sensitivity and realism on the part of the giver, and an open-mindedness and willingness to learn from the receiver. Boud et al. (1993, pp 204–205) offer the following guidance on giving and receiving feedback.

Useful **information**

9.3 Giving feedback

Giving feedback
Be realistic – your comments should relate only to things that the learner has the power to change.
Be specific – base your comments on concrete observable behaviour or outcomes and give clear examples.
Be sensitive to the goals of the other person – these may be different from yours and your comments will need to recognise this and take them into account.
Be timely – give feedback promptly, and at a time when the other person is likely to be receptive.
Be descriptive – you should be clear and descriptive in what you say, not evaluative or emotionally manipulative, so the other person can decide whether to accept what you say or not.
Be consciously non-judgemental – offer your personal view (eg 'I feel that …') without making value-laden statements.
Don't compare – each piece of feedback relates to an individual person in a specific context, and does not compare to others in other contexts.
Be diligent – make sure what you are saying is accurate and reflects what you want to say.
Be direct – say what you mean without wrapping it up in fancy words or abstract language.
Be positive – say what you appreciate as well as saying where there is room for improvement, and make this a genuine response rather than saying something positive because it is required or expected.
Be aware – check your own emotional state before you give feedback so that your focus can be on the other person and not yourself.

Source: Boud et al., 1985

Useful **information**

9.4 Receiving feedback

Receiving feedback
Be explicit – make it clear what kind of feedback you are seeking and, if necessary, what you do not want to receive.
Be attentive – concentrate on what is being said and on what the other person wants you to know, not on what you want to hear.
Be aware – notice your own reactions, both intellectual and emotional, and note if you are tending to reject the feedback because the other person's viewpoint differs from yours.
Be silent – try and stop yourself from making a response or even considering a response until you have received all the feedback and considered the implications. If you feel you need to explain, wait until after the feedback session when you have had time to consider and attend to all that has been said.

Source: Boud et al., 1985

Chapter **summary**

Summative assessment for social workers will be framed by the KSS for children and families sector as practitioners work towards accredited status, and the HCPC Standards of Proficiency for all registered social workers until a new regulator is established. These set out the threshold standards for safe practice, the outcomes for the qualifying level set out in the PCF, and the knowledge and skills required at different levels/phases of a social worker's career and practice experience. Most universities will use a portfolio for at least some parts of the learning programme; this may be in relation to key skills, to preparation for placement, for independent study modules or for practice placements.

Employers will also rely on a form of portfolio for assessing newly qualified social workers on their ASYE and in all likelihood for demonstrating the evidence for employer endorsement for children and families social workers looking to gain approved status via the national testing scheme. During their programme, social workers will be asked to gather evidence of how their practice demonstrates that they have met the PCF outcomes at ASYE level. This is likely to involve them in developing a learning agreement with their employers, keeping records of their practice and their learning activities, and writing reflective accounts of how their learning and practice have developed. Supervision sessions will give formative feedback which can again be used to show how a learning need is being identified and addressed. At the end of the programme, the employer will be asked to review all this evidence and make a judgement about whether the ASYE outcomes have been met.

The highest stakes assessment which social workers are likely to meet after their initial qualification is when they come to re-register with the HCPC. In order to remain registered, social workers will need to show that they have continued to engage in professional development since their last registration. The HCPC website (www.hpc-uk.org/registrants) gives substantial guidance on registration and re-registration and CPD requirements. We have said more about what the requirements are and how you can show that you are meeting them in Chapter 7. The HCPC employs experienced professionals who will review the evidence you provide in relation to their standards. If you have maintained your portfolio along the lines that we have suggested in this book, you should have no trouble extracting from it evidence that is relevant and effective in bringing about improved outcomes for service users.

Final thoughts

We hope that you now have a good idea about what portfolios are, why they are useful for learning and how they can be used to support professional development and to demonstrate achievement. We have included a final checklist in Appendix 6 to help you to work through developing, assessing and reviewing portfolios. It suggests what needs to be done, what action this implies at each stage, and who should be involved in each action. The range of types and purposes of portfolios in use and under development means that in specific circumstances only some stages will be appropriate, and the terminology for those involved in supporting and assessing will vary from scheme to scheme. However, Appendix 6 may act as a framework within which to begin to develop a portfolio, whether you approach the process as a learner, an assessor or a manager.

References

Angehrn, A.A (2004) Learning by Playing: Bridging the Knowing-Doing Gap in Urban Communities, in Bounfour, A. and Edvinsson, L. (eds) *Intellectual Capital for Communities: Nations, Regions, Districts, Cities.* Boston, MA: Butterworth-Heinemann.

Angehrn, A.A. (2005a) Designing Innovation Games for Community-based Learning & Knowledge Exchange. *International Journal of Knowledge & Learning*, 1: 15–29.

Angehrn, A.A. (2005b) Learning to Manage Innovation and Change through Organizational and People Dynamics Simulations. *International Simulation & Gaming Association Conference (ISAGA 05).* Atlanta, GA.

Askeland, G.A. and Fook, J. (2009) Critical Reflection in Social Work. *European Journal of Social Work*, 12: 287–292.

Baume, D. (2001) *A Briefing on Assessment of Portfolios.* York: Learning and Teaching Support Network.

Boud, D., Cohen, R. and Walker, D. (1993) *Using Experience for Learning.* Buckingham: SRHE/The Open University.

Boud, D., Keogh, R. and Walker, D. (1985) *Reflection: Turning Experience into Learning.* London: Kegan Paul.

Brennan, J. and Little, B. (1996) *A Review of Work Based Learning in Higher Education.* Great Britain: Department for Education and Employment.

Brown, K., Keen, S., Rutter, L. and Warren, A. (2010) *Partnerships, Continuing Professional Development (CPD) and the Accreditation of Prior Learning (APL): Supporting Workforce Development across the Social Care Sector.* Birmingham: Learn to Care.

Challis, M. (1993) *Introducing APEL.* London: Routledge.

Challis, M. (1999) AMEE Medical Education Guide No 11 (revised): Portfolio Based Learning and Assessment in Medical Education. *Med Teacher*, 21: 370–386.

Challis, M., Mathers, N.J., Howe, A.C. and Field, N. (1997) Portfolio Based Learning: Continuing Medical Education for General Practitioners – a Mid-point Evaluation. *Medical Education*, 31: 22–66.

DfE (Department for Education) (2014) *Knowledge and Skills Statement for Child and Family Social Workers.* London: TSO.

DfE (2015) *Knowledge and Skills Statement for Practice Supervisors and Practice Leaders.* London: TSO.

DH (Department of Health) (2006) *Options for Excellence: Building the Social Care Workforce of the Future.* London: The Stationery Office.

DH (2015) *Knowledge and Skills Statement for Adult Social Workers.* London: TSO.

Dickens, J. (2011) Social Work in England at a Watershed – as Always: From the Seebohm Report to the Social Work Task Force. *British Journal of Social Work*, 41: 22–39.

Drew, S. and Bingham, R. (2001) *The Student Skills Guide.* Aldershot: Gower.

Driessen, E. (2008) *Educating the Self-critical Doctor: Using a Portfolio to Stimulate and Assess Medical Students' Reflection.* Maastricht: University of Maastricht.

Eraut, M. (1994) *Developing Professional Knowledge and Competence.* London: Falmer.

Fook, J. and Askeland, G.A. (2007) Challenges of Critical Reflection: Nothing Ventured, Nothing Gained. *Social Work Education*, iFirst Article: 1–13.

Fook, J. and Gardner, F. (2012) *Critical Reflection in Context: Applications in Health & Social Care.* Abingdon: Routledge.

Gardner, F. and Fook, J. (2012) *Using Critical Reflection in Health and Social Care: A Case Study-based Introduction*. Abingdon: Routledge.

Gibbs, G. (1992) *Improving the Quality of Student Learning*. Bristol: Technical & Education Services Ltd.

Graham, J. (1989) Portfolios and Their Implications for Portability in Modular Schemes. *Journal of In Service Education*, 18: 46–50.

GSCC (General Social Care Council) (2005) *Registration Rules 2003* (amended 2005). London: GSCC.

Hall, D. (1992) Professional Development Portfolios for Teachers and Lecturers. *Journal of In Service Education*, 18: 81–86.

HCPC (Health & Care Professions Council) (2012a) *Continuing Professional Development* [Online]. Available at: www.hpc-uk.org/registrants/cpd/index.asp (Accessed 20 December 2012).

HCPC (2012b) *Standards of Proficiency – Social Workers in England* [Online]. Available at: www.hpc-uk.org/publications/standards/index.asp?id=569 (Accessed 20 December 2012).

Honey, P. and Mumford, A. (1992) *The Manual of Learning Styles*. Maidenhead: P. Honey.

JISC (Joint Information Systems Committee) (2008) *Effective Practice with e-Portfolios* [Online]. Available at: www.jisc.ac.uk/whatwedo/programmes/elearning/~/link.aspx?_id=272842BD23554CBF9CD993169D943EC4&_z=z (Accessed 20 December 2012).

JISC (2012) *Crossing the Threshold: Moving e-Portfolios into the Mainstream* [Online]. Available at: www.jisc.ac.uk/media/documents/programmes/elearning/eportfolios/threshold.pdf (Accessed 21 December 2012).

Knight, P. (2006) The Local Practices of Assessment. *Assessment & Evaluation in Higher Education*, 31: 435–452.

Knowles, M. (1970) Andragogy: An Emerging Technology for Adult Learning, in Tight, M. (ed) *Education for Adults: Adult Learning and Education*. London: Croom Helm.

Kolb, D.A. (1984) *Experiential Learning: Experience as the Source of Learning and Development*. Englewood Cliffs/London: Prentice-Hall.

Lewin, K. (1942) Field Theory and Learning, in Cartwright, D. (ed) *Field Theory in Social Science: Selected Theoretical Papers*. 1951 edn. New York and London: Harper and Row.

LGA (Local Government Association) (2015) *Standards for Employers and Supervision* [Online]. Available at: www.local.gov.uk/documents/10180/6188796/The_standards_for_employers_of_social_workers.pdf/fb7cb809-650c-4ccd-8aa7-fecb07271c4a.

Marton, F. and Saljo, R. (1984) Approaches to Learning, in Marton, F., Hounsell, D. and Entwistle, N.J. (eds) *The Experience of Learning*. Edinburgh: Scottish Academic Press.

Munro, E. and Great Britain Department for Education (2011) *The Munro Review of Child Protection Final Report: A Child-centred System*. Cm (Series) (Great Britain Parliament) 8062 2010–11. Norwich: The Stationery Office.

NCVQ (National Council for Vocational Qualifications) (1991) *Guide to National Vocational Qualifications*. London: NCVQ.

NMC (Nursing and Midwifery Council) (2012) *The Prep Handbook*. London: NMC.

Payne, M. (2005) *The Origins of Social Work: Continuity and Change*. Basingstoke: Palgrave Macmillan.

Piaget, J., Tomlinson, A. and Tomlinson, J. (1929) *The Child's Conception of the World*. Savage, MD: Rowman & Littlefield.

QAA (Quality Assurance Agency) (2008) *Higher Education Credit Framework for England: Guidance on Academic Credit Arrangements in Higher Education in England*. London: QAA/Universities UK.

Redman, W. (1994) *Portfolios for Development*. London: Kegan Paul.

Riegel, K.F. (1973) Dialectic Operations: The Final Period of Cognitive Development. *Human Development*, 16: 346–370.

Schön, D.A. (1987) *Educating the Reflective Practitioner*. San Francisco, CA: Jossey-Bass.

Schön, D.A. (1991) *The Reflective Practitioner: How Professionals Think in Action*. Aldershot: Avebury.

Simosko, S. (1991) *APL: A Practical Guide for Professionals*. London: Kogan Page.

Snadden, D. and Thomas, M. (1996) *Bringing Education to Training: Final Report and Appendices*. Tayside: Tayside Centre for General Practice.

SWTF (Social Work Task Force) (2009) *Building a Safe, Confident Future: The Final Report of the Social Work Task Force, November 2009*. London: Department for Children, Schools and Families.

TCSW (The College of Social Work) (2012a) *Assessing Practice Using the Professional Capabilities Framework* [out of publication].

TCSW (2012b) *ASYE1: Understanding What Is Meant by Holistic Assessment* [Online]. Available at: www.basw.co.uk/resource/?id=4789.

TCSW (2012c) *CPD1 – The Future of Continuing Professional Development (CPD)* [Online]. Available at: www.basw.co.uk/resource/?id=1170.

TCSW (2012d) *Developing Your Social Work Practice Using the PCF: Integrated Critical Analysis and Reflective Practice* [out of publication].

TCSW (2012e) *Holistic Assessment Toolkits* [out of publication].

TCSW (2012f) *Professional Capabilities Framework (PCF)* [Online]. Available at: www.basw.co.uk/resource/?id=1137 (Accessed 20 December 2012).

TCSW (2012g) *Progression between Levels* [Online]. Available at: www.collegeofsocialwork.org/pcf.aspx (Accessed 3 March 2013).

Tosh, D. and Werdmuller, B. (2004) *ePortfolios and Weblogs: One Vision for ePortfolio Development* [out of publication].

Usherwood, T., Challis, M. and Joesbury, H. (1994) Towards Competence Based Assessment. *Innovative Learning and Assessment, Sharing Ideas,* 3. London: Kings Fund.

Webster-Wright, A. (2009) Reframing Professional Development through Understanding Authentic Professional Learning. *Review of Educational Research*, 79: 702–739.

Appendix 1: PCF domains and capabilities

© TCSW, 2012

The capabilities in each domain at each level are set out in this appendix for reference purposes but it should be remembered that the PCF is designed to be applied holistically. You will not need to evidence every single capability statement at your level, but rather your portfolio should provide a view across capabilities with plans and activities mapped to different domain areas (for further details see TCSW, 2012f).

Level: end of last placement

Professionalism

Social workers are members of an internationally recognised profession, a title protected in UK law. Social workers demonstrate professional commitment by taking responsibility for their conduct, practice and learning, with support through supervision. As representatives of the social work profession they safeguard its reputation and are accountable to the professional regulator.

- » Be able to meet the requirements of the professional regulator.
- » Be able to explain the role of the social worker in a range of contexts, and uphold the reputation of the profession.
- » Demonstrate an effective and active use of supervision for accountability, professional reflection and development.
- » Demonstrate professionalism in terms of presentation, demeanour, reliability, honesty and respectfulness.
- » Take responsibility for managing your time and workload effectively, and begin to prioritise your activity including supervision time.
- » Recognise the impact of self in interaction with others, making appropriate use of personal experience.
- » Be able to recognise and maintain personal and professional boundaries.
- » Recognise your professional limitations and how to seek advice.
- » Demonstrate a commitment to your continuing learning and development.
- » With support, take steps to manage and promote own safety, health, wellbeing and emotional resilience.

» Identify concerns about practice and procedures and, with support, begin to find appropriate means of challenge.

Values and ethics

Social workers have an obligation to conduct themselves ethically and to engage in ethical decision making, including through partnership with people who use their services. Social workers are knowledgeable about the value base of their profession, its ethical standards and relevant law.

» Understand and apply the profession's ethical principles and legislation, taking account of these in reaching decisions.

» Recognise and, with support, manage the impact of own values on professional practice.

» Manage potentially conflicting or competing values, and, with guidance, recognise, reflect on and work with ethical dilemmas.

» Demonstrate respectful partnership work with service users and carers, eliciting and respecting their needs and views, and promoting their participation in decision making wherever possible.

» Recognise and promote individuals' rights to autonomy and self-determination.

» Promote and protect the privacy of individuals within and outside their families and networks, recognising the requirements of professional accountability and information sharing.

Diversity

Social workers understand that diversity characterises and shapes human experience and is critical to the formation of identity. Diversity is multi-dimensional and includes race, disability, class, economic status, age, sexuality, gender and transgender, faith and belief. Social workers appreciate that, as a consequence of difference, a person's life experience may include oppression, marginalisation and alienation as well as privilege, power and acclaim, and are able to challenge appropriately.

» Understand how an individual's identity is informed by factors such as culture, economic status, family composition, life experiences and characteristics, and take account of these to understand their experiences, questioning assumptions where necessary.

» With reference to current legislative requirements, recognise personal and organisational discrimination and oppression and with guidance make use of a range of approaches to challenge them.

» Recognise and manage the impact on people of the power invested in your role.

Rights, justice and economic wellbeing

Social workers recognise the fundamental principles of human rights and equality, and that these are protected in national and international law, conventions and policies. They ensure these principles underpin their practice. Social workers understand the importance of using and contributing to case law and applying these rights in their own practice. They understand the effects of oppression, discrimination and poverty.

» Understand, identify and apply in practice the principles of social justice, inclusion and equality.

» Understand how legislation and guidance can advance or constrain people's rights and recognise how the law may be used to protect or advance their rights and entitlements.

» Work within the principles of human and civil rights and equalities legislation, differentiating and beginning to work with absolute, qualified and competing rights and differing needs and perspectives.

» Recognise the impact of poverty and social exclusion and promote enhanced economic status through access to education, work, housing, health services and welfare benefits.

» Recognise the value of – and aid access to – independent advocacy.

Knowledge

Social workers understand psychological, social, cultural, spiritual and physical influences on people; human development throughout the life span and the legal framework for practice. They apply this knowledge in their work with individuals, families and communities. They know and use theories and methods of social work practice.

» Demonstrate a critical understanding of the application to social work of research, theory and knowledge from sociology, social policy, psychology and health.

» Demonstrate a critical understanding of the legal and policy frameworks and guidance that inform and mandate social work practice, recognising the scope for professional judgement.

» Demonstrate and apply to practice a working knowledge of human growth and development throughout the life course.

» Recognise the short- and long-term impact of psychological, socio-economic, environmental and physiological factors on people's lives, taking into account age and development, and how this informs practice.

» Recognise how systemic approaches can be used to understand the person-in-the-environment and inform your practice.

» Acknowledge the centrality of relationships for people and the key concepts of attachment, separation, loss, change and resilience.

» Understand forms of harm and their impact on people, and the implications for practice, drawing on concepts of strength, resilience, vulnerability, risk and resistance, and apply to practice.

» Demonstrate a critical knowledge of the range of theories and models for social work intervention with individuals, families, groups and communities, and the methods derived from them.

» Demonstrate a critical understanding of social welfare policy, its evolution, implementation and impact on people, social work, other professions and inter-agency working.

» Recognise the contribution, and begin to make use, of research to inform practice.

» Demonstrate a critical understanding of research methods.

» Value and take account of the expertise of service users, carers and professionals.

Critical reflection and analysis

Social workers are knowledgeable about and apply the principles of critical thinking and reasoned discernment. They identify, distinguish, evaluate and integrate multiple sources of knowledge and evidence. These include practice evidence, their own practice experience, service user and carer experience together with research-based, organisational, policy and legal knowledge. They use critical thinking augmented by creativity and curiosity.

» Apply imagination, creativity and curiosity to practice.

» Inform decision making through the identification and gathering of information from multiple sources, actively seeking new sources.

» With support, rigorously question and evaluate the reliability and validity of information from different sources.

» Demonstrate a capacity for logical, systematic, critical and reflective reasoning and apply the theories and techniques of reflective practice.

» Know how to formulate, test, evaluate and review hypotheses in response to information available at the time and apply in practice.

» Begin to formulate and make explicit, evidence-informed judgements and justifiable decisions.

Intervention and skills

Social workers engage with individuals, families, groups and communities, working alongside people to assess and intervene. They enable effective relationships and are effective communicators, using appropriate skills. Using their professional judgement, they employ a range of interventions: promoting independence, providing support and protection, taking preventative action and ensuring safety whilst balancing rights and risks. They understand and take account of differentials in power, and are able to use authority appropriately. They evaluate their own practice and the outcomes for those they work with.

» Identify and apply a range of verbal, non-verbal and written methods of communication and adapt them in line with people's age, comprehension and culture.

» Be able to communicate information, advice, instruction and professional opinion so as to advocate, influence and persuade.

» Demonstrate the ability to engage with people, and build, manage, sustain and conclude compassionate and effective relationships.

» Demonstrate an holistic approach to the identification of needs, circumstances, rights, strengths and risks.

» Select and use appropriate frameworks to assess, give meaning to, plan, implement and review effective interventions and evaluate the outcomes, in partnership with service users.

» Use a planned and structured approach, informed by social work methods, models and tools, to promote positive change and independence and to prevent harm.

» Recognise how the development of community resources, groups and networks enhances outcomes for individuals.

» Maintain accurate, comprehensible, succinct and timely records and reports in accordance with applicable legislation, protocols and guidelines, to support professional judgement and organisational responsibilities.

» Demonstrate skills in sharing information appropriately and respectfully.

» Recognise complexity, multiple factors, changing circumstances and uncertainty in people's lives, to be able to prioritise your intervention.

» Understand the authority of the social work role and begin to use this appropriately as an accountable professional.

» Recognise the factors that create or exacerbate risk to individuals, their families or carers, to the public or to professionals, including yourself, and contribute to the assessment and management of risk.

» With support, identify appropriate responses to safeguard vulnerable people and promote their wellbeing.

Contexts and organisations

Social workers are informed about and proactively responsive to the challenges and opportunities that come with changing social contexts and constructs. They fulfil this responsibility in accordance with their professional values and ethics, both as individual professionals and as members of the organisation in which they work. They collaborate, inform and are informed by their work with others, inter-professionally and with communities.

» Recognise that social work operates within, and responds to, changing economic, social, political and organisational contexts.

» Understand the roles and responsibilities of social workers in a range of organisations, lines of accountability and the boundaries of professional autonomy and discretion.

» Understand legal obligations, structures and behaviours within organisations and how these impact on policy, procedure and practice.

» Be able to work within an organisation's remit and contribute to its evaluation and development.

» Understand and respect the role of others within the organisation and work effectively with them.

» Take responsibility for your role and impact within teams and be able to contribute positively to effective team working.

» Understand the inter-agency, multi-disciplinary and inter-professional dimensions to practice and demonstrate effective partnership working.

Professional leadership

The social work profession evolves through the contribution of its members in activities such as practice research, supervision, assessment of practice, teaching and management. An individual's contribution will gain influence when undertaken as part of a learning, practice-focused organisation. Learning may be facilitated with a wide range of people including social work colleagues, service users and carers, volunteers, foster carers and other professionals.

» Recognise the importance of, and begin to demonstrate, professional leadership as a social worker.

» Recognise the value of, and contribute to supporting the learning and development of others.

Level: Assessed and Supported Year in Employment (ASYE)

Professionalism

Social workers are members of an internationally recognised profession, a title protected in UK law. Social workers demonstrate professional commitment by taking responsibility for their conduct, practice and learning, with support through supervision. As representatives of the social work profession they safeguard its reputation and are accountable to the professional regulator.

> » Be able to meet the requirements of the professional regulator.

> » Be able to explain the role of the social worker in a range of contexts, and uphold the reputation of the profession.

> » Make proactive use of supervision to reflect critically on practice, explore different approaches to your work, support your development across the nine capabilities and understand the boundaries of professional accountability.

> » Demonstrate workload management skills and develop the ability to prioritise.

> » Recognise and balance your own personal/professional boundaries in response to changing and more complex contexts.

> » Demonstrate professionalism in terms of presentation, demeanour, reliability, honesty and respectfulness.

> » Demonstrate workload management skills and develop the ability to prioritise.

> » Recognise and balance your own personal/professional boundaries in response to changing and more complex contexts.

> » Identify your learning needs; assume responsibility for improving your practice through appropriate professional development.

> » Develop ways to promote wellbeing at work, identifying strategies to protect and promote your own wellbeing and the wellbeing of others.

> » Identify and implement strategies for responding appropriately to concerns about practice or procedures, seeking guidance if required.

Values and ethics

Social workers have an obligation to conduct themselves ethically and to engage in ethical decision making, including through partnership with people who use their services. Social workers are knowledgeable about the value base of their profession, its ethical standards and relevant law.

> » Understand and apply the profession's ethical principles and legislation, taking account of these in reaching decisions.

> » Recognise and manage the impact of your own values on professional practice.

> » Recognise and manage conflicting values and ethical dilemmas to arrive at principled decisions.

> » Demonstrate respectful partnership work with service users and carers, eliciting and respecting their needs and views, and promoting their participation in decision making wherever possible.

» Recognise and promote individuals' rights to autonomy and self-determination.

» Promote and protect the privacy of individuals within and outside their families and networks, recognising the requirements of professional accountability and information sharing.

Diversity

Social workers understand that diversity characterises and shapes human experience and is critical to the formation of identity. Diversity is multi-dimensional and includes race, disability, class, economic status, age, sexuality, gender and transgender, faith and belief. Social workers appreciate that, as a consequence of difference, a person's life experience may include oppression, marginalisation and alienation as well as privilege, power and acclaim, and are able to challenge appropriately.

» Identify and take account of the significance of diversity and discrimination on the lives of people, and show application of this understanding in your practice.

» Recognise oppression and discrimination by individuals or organisations and implement appropriate strategies to challenge.

» Identify the impact of the power invested in your role on relationships and your intervention, and be able to adapt your practice accordingly.

Rights, justice and economic wellbeing

Social workers recognise the fundamental principles of human rights and equality, and that these are protected in national and international law, conventions and policies. They ensure these principles underpin their practice. Social workers understand the importance of using and contributing to case law and applying these rights in their own practice. They understand the effects of oppression, discrimination and poverty.

» Begin to integrate principles of and entitlements to social justice, social inclusion and equality in your analysis and practice, by identifying factors that contribute to inequality and exclusion, and supporting people to pursue options to enhance their wellbeing.

» Address oppression and discrimination, applying the law to protect and advance people's rights, recognising how legislation can constrain or advance these rights.

» Apply in practice principles of human, civil rights and equalities legislation, and manage competing rights, differing needs and perspectives.

» Recognise the impact of poverty and social exclusion and promote enhanced economic status through access to education, work, housing, health services and welfare benefit.

» Empower service users through recognising their rights and enable access where appropriate to independent advocacy.

Knowledge

Social workers understand psychological, social, cultural, spiritual and physical influences on people; human development throughout the life span and the legal framework for practice. They apply this knowledge in their work with individuals, families and communities. They know and use theories and methods of social work practice.

» Consolidate, develop and demonstrate comprehensive understanding and application of the knowledge gained in your initial training, and knowledge related to your specialist area of practice, including critical awareness of current issues and new evidence-based practice research.

» Demonstrate knowledge and application of appropriate legal and policy frameworks and guidance that inform and mandate social work practice. Apply legal reasoning, using professional legal expertise and advice appropriately, recognising where scope for professional judgement exists.

» Demonstrate and apply to practice a working knowledge of human growth and development throughout the life course.

» Recognise the short- and long-term impact of psychological, socio-economic, environmental and physiological factors on people's lives, taking into account age and development, and how this informs practice.

» Recognise how systemic approaches can be used to understand the person-in-the-environment and inform your practice.

» Acknowledge the centrality of relationships for people and the key concepts of attachment, separation, loss, change and resilience.

» Understand forms of harm and their impact on people, and the implications for practice, drawing on concepts of strength, resilience, vulnerability, risk and resistance, and apply to practice.

» Demonstrate a critical knowledge of the range of theories and models for social work intervention with individuals, families, groups and communities, and the methods derived from them.

» Demonstrate a critical understanding of social welfare policy, its evolution, implementation and impact on people, social work, other professions and inter-agency working.

» Recognise the contribution, and begin to make use, of research to inform practice.

» Demonstrate a critical understanding of research methods.

» Value and take account of the expertise of service users, carers and professionals.

Critical reflection and analysis

Social workers are knowledgeable about and apply the principles of critical thinking and reasoned discernment. They identify, distinguish, evaluate and integrate multiple sources of knowledge and evidence. These include practice evidence, their own practice experience, service user and carer experience together with research-based, organisational, policy and legal knowledge. They use critical thinking augmented by creativity and curiosity.

> » Show creativity in tackling and solving problems, by considering a range of options to solve dilemmas.

> » Use reflective practice techniques to evaluate and critically analyse information, gained from a variety of sources, to construct and test hypotheses and make explicit evidence-informed decisions.

Intervention and skills

Social workers engage with individuals, families, groups and communities, working alongside people to assess and intervene. They enable effective relationships and are effective communicators, using appropriate skills. Using their professional judgement, they employ a range of interventions: promoting independence, providing support and protection, taking preventative action and ensuring safety whilst balancing rights and risks. They understand and take account of differentials in power, and are able to use authority appropriately. They evaluate their own practice and the outcomes for those they work with.

> » Use a range of methods to engage and communicate effectively with service users, eliciting the needs, wishes and feelings of all those involved, taking account of situations where these are not explicitly expressed.

> » Demonstrate clear communication of evidence-based professional reasoning, judgements and decisions, to professional and non-professional audiences.

> » Build and use effective relationships with a wide range of people, networks, communities and professionals to improve outcomes, showing an ability to manage resistance.

> » Use appropriate assessment frameworks, applying information-gathering skills to make and contribute to assessments, whilst continuing to build relationships and offer support.

> » Select, use and review appropriate and timely social work interventions, informed by evidence of their effectiveness, that are best suited to the service user(s), family, carer, setting and self.

> » Use a planned and structured approach, informed by social work methods, models and tools, to promote positive change and independence and to prevent harm.

» Recognise how the development of community resources, groups and networks enhances outcomes for individuals.

» Record information in a timely, respectful and accurate manner. Write records and reports, for a variety of purposes with language suited to function, using information management systems. Distinguish fact from opinion, and record conflicting views and perspectives.

» Share information consistently in ways that meet legal, ethical and agency requirements.

» Recognise complexity, multiple factors, changing circumstances and uncertainty in people's lives, be able to prioritise your intervention.

» Use authority appropriately in your role.

» Demonstrate understanding of and respond to risk factors in your practice. Contribute to the assessment and management of risk, including strategies for reducing risk, distinguishing levels of risk for different situations.

» Demonstrate application of principles and practice for safeguarding adults and children including consideration of potential abuse. Apply strategies that aim to reduce and prevent harm and abuse.

Contexts and organisations

Social workers are informed about and proactively responsive to the challenges and opportunities that come with changing social contexts and constructs. They fulfil this responsibility in accordance with their professional values and ethics, both as individual professionals and as members of the organisation in which they work. They collaborate, inform and are informed by their work with others, inter-professionally and with communities.

» Taking account of legal, operational and policy contexts, proactively engage with your own organisation and contribute to its evaluation and development.

» Proactively engage with colleagues, and a range of organisations to identify, assess, plan and support the needs of service users and communities.

» Understand legal obligations, structures and behaviours within organisations and how these impact on policy, procedure and practice.

» Be able to work within an organisation's remit and contribute to its evaluation and development.

» Understand and respect the role of others within the organisation and work effectively with them.

» Work effectively as a member of a team, demonstrating the ability to develop and maintain appropriate professional and inter-professional relationships, managing challenge and conflict with support.

Professional leadership

The social work profession evolves through the contribution of its members in activities such as practice research, supervision, assessment of practice, teaching and management. An individual's contribution will gain influence when undertaken as part of a learning, practice-focused organisation. Learning may be facilitated with a wide range of people including social work colleagues, service users and carers, volunteers, foster carers and other professionals.

» Show the capacity for leading practice through the manner in which you conduct your professional role, your contribution to supervision and to team meetings.

» Take steps to enable the learning and development of others.

Level: social worker

Professionalism

Social workers are members of an internationally recognised profession, a title protected in UK law. Social workers demonstrate professional commitment by taking responsibility for their conduct, practice and learning, with support through supervision. As representatives of the social work profession they safeguard its reputation and are accountable to the professional regulator.

» Be able to meet the requirements of the professional regulator.

» Promote the profession in a growing range of contexts.

» Take responsibility for obtaining regular, effective supervision from an SW [social worker] for effective practice, reflection and career development.

» Maintain professionalism in the face of more challenging circumstances.

» Manage workload independently, seeking support and suggesting solutions for workload difficulties.

» Maintain appropriate personal/professional boundaries in more challenging circumstances.

» Make skilled use of self as part of your interventions.

» Maintain awareness of own professional limitations and knowledge gaps. Establish a network of internal and external colleagues from whom to seek advice and expertise.

> » Identify and act on learning needs for CPD, including
>
>> » through supervision;
>>
>> » routinely promote wellbeing at work;
>>
>> » raise and address issues of poor practice, internally through the organisation, and then independently if required.

Values and ethics

Social workers have an obligation to conduct themselves ethically and to engage in ethical decision making, including through partnership with people who use their services. Social workers are knowledgeable about the value base of their profession, its ethical standards and relevant law.

> » Demonstrate confident application of ethical reasoning to professional practice, rights and entitlements, questioning and challenging others using a legal and human rights framework.
>
> » Critically reflect on and manage the influence and impact of own and others' values on professional practice.
>
> » Recognise and manage conflicting values and ethical dilemmas, in practice, using supervision and team discussion, questioning and challenging others, including those from other professions.
>
> » Negotiate and establish boundaries to underpin partnership work with service users, carers and their networks, using transparency and honesty.
>
> » Ensure practice is underpinned by policy, procedures and code of conduct to promote individuals' rights to determine their own solutions, promoting problem-solving skills, whilst recognising how and when self-determination may be constrained (by the law).
>
> » Work to protect privacy and promote trust, whilst being able to justify, explain and take appropriate action when the right to privacy is over-ridden by professional or legal requirements.

Diversity

Social workers understand that diversity characterises and shapes human experience and is critical to the formation of identity. Diversity is multi-dimensional and includes race, disability, class, economic status, age, sexuality, gender and transgender, faith and belief. Social workers appreciate that, as a consequence of difference, a person's life experience may include oppression, marginalisation and alienation as well as privilege, power and acclaim, and are able to challenge appropriately.

» Recognise the complexity of identity and diversity of experience, and apply this to practice.

» Recognise discriminatory practices and develop a range of approaches to appropriately challenge service users, colleagues and senior staff.

» Critically reflect on and manage the power of your role in your relationship with others.

Rights, justice and economic wellbeing

Social workers recognise the fundamental principles of human rights and equality, and that these are protected in national and international law, conventions and policies. They ensure these principles underpin their practice. Social workers understand the importance of using and contributing to case law and applying these rights in their own practice. They understand the effects of oppression, discrimination and poverty.

» Routinely integrate the principles of and entitlements to social justice, social inclusion and equality, and with support, consider how and when challenge may be needed.

» Routinely apply the law to protect and advance people's rights and entitlements, identifying and highlighting situations where interpretations of the law are neither proportionate nor fair to promote autonomy and self-determination.

» Apply the principles and entitlements of human and civil rights to analyse, evaluate and challenge interventions that are unlawful and/or disproportionate.

» Analyse differing needs, perspectives and competing rights and apply to practice.

» Enable and support people to consider and pursue a range of options that may enhance economic status (through access to education, work, housing, health services and welfare benefits).

» Where appropriate, set up and/or enable access to effective independent advocacy.

Knowledge

Social workers understand psychological, social, cultural, spiritual and physical influences on people; human development throughout the life span and the legal framework for practice. They apply this knowledge in their work with individuals, families and communities. They know and use theories and methods of social work practice.

» Demonstrate a comprehensive understanding and use of knowledge related to your area of practice, including critical awareness of current issues and new evidence-based practice research.

» Demonstrate knowledge and application of appropriate legal and policy frameworks and guidance that inform and mandate social work practice. Apply legal reasoning, using professional legal expertise and advice appropriately, recognising where scope for professional judgement exists.

» Demonstrate and apply to practice a working knowledge of human growth and development throughout the life course.

» Recognise the short- and long-term impact of psychological, socio-economic, environmental and physiological factors on people's lives, taking into account age and development, and how this informs practice.

» Recognise how systemic approaches can be used to understand the person-in-the-environment and inform your practice.

» Acknowledge the centrality of relationships for people and the key concepts of attachment, separation, loss, change and resilience.

» Understand forms of harm and their impact on people, and the implications for practice, drawing on concepts of strength, resilience, vulnerability, risk and resistance, and apply to practice.

» Demonstrate a critical knowledge of the range of theories and models for social work intervention with individuals, families, groups and communities, and the methods derived from them.

» Demonstrate a critical understanding of social welfare policy, its evolution, implementation and impact on people, social work, other professions and inter-agency working.

» Recognise the contribution, and begin to make use, of research to inform practice.

» Demonstrate a critical understanding of research methods.

» Value and take account of the expertise of service users, carers and professionals.

Critical reflection and analysis

The following capability pathways apply.

» Routinely and efficiently apply critical reflection and analysis to increasingly complex cases.

» Draw on a wide range of evidence sources to inform decision making.

» Ensure hypotheses and options are reviewed to inform judgement and decision making.

» Start to provide professional opinion.

Intervention and skills

Social workers engage with individuals, families, groups and communities, working alongside people to assess and intervene. They enable effective relationships and are effective communicators, using appropriate skills. Using their professional judgement, they employ a range of interventions: promoting independence, providing support and protection, taking preventative action and ensuring safety whilst balancing rights and risks. They understand and take account of differentials in power, and are able to use authority appropriately. They evaluate their own practice and the outcomes for those they work with.

>> Communicate with compassion and authority in challenging situations and with resistant individuals.

>> Routinely explain professional reasoning, judgements and decisions.

>> Engage effectively with people in complex situations, both short term and building relationships over time.

>> Gather information so as to inform judgement for interventions in more complex situations and in response to challenge.

>> Use assessment procedures discerningly so as to inform judgement.

>> Develop a range of interventions; use them effectively and evaluate them in practice.

>> Expand intervention methods and demonstrate expertise in one or more specific methods relevant to your setting.

>> Make timely decisions when positive change is not happening.

>> Actively support and initiate community groups and networks, including professional ones.

>> Clearly report and record analysis and judgements.

>> Demonstrate and promote appropriate information sharing.

>> Use contingency planning to anticipate complexity and changing circumstances.

>> Recognise and appropriately manage the authority inherent in your position.

>> Demonstrate confident and effective judgement about risk and accountability in your decisions.

>> Regularly undertake assessment and planning for safeguarding.

Contexts and organisations

The following capability pathways apply.

>> Keep abreast of changing context at local and national level, and take account of these in practice.

» Demonstrate the ability to work within your own organisation, and identify and begin to work with the relationship between the organisation, practice and wider changing contexts.

» Work to and explain the relevant legal structures in the organisation, including basic case law; know when and how to access support and appropriate legal advice and consultation.

» Explore and identify how organisational practice can support good social work practice.

» Keep abreast of changing roles in the organisation; recognise, value and engage with other specialist perspectives.

» Be confident about your role in the team, working positively with others; draw on and contribute to team working and collaborative support wherever possible.

» Take an active role in inter-professional and inter-agency work, building own network and collaborative working.

Professional leadership

The following capability pathways apply.

» Contribute to and promote the development of practice, taking the initiative to test new approaches.

» Contribute to the learning of others.

» Practice Educator Standards Stage 1: Domain A, B, C.

Level: experienced social worker

Professionalism

Social workers are members of an internationally recognised profession, a title protected in UK law. Social workers demonstrate professional commitment by taking responsibility for their conduct, practice and learning, with support through supervision. As representatives of the social work profession they safeguard its reputation and are accountable to the professional regulator.

» Be able to meet the requirements of the professional regulator.

» Model the social work role, set expectations for others and contribute to the public face of the organisation.

» Expect supervision that covers practice, organisational and management aspects of role, applying critical reflection throughout.

» Model and help others to demonstrate professionalism.

» Model and help others with effective workload management skills.

» Model and help others to maintain professional/personal boundaries and skilled use of self.

» Maintain awareness of own professional limitations and knowledge gaps. Establish a network of internal and external colleagues from whom to seek advice and expertise.

» Contribute to a learning environment for self, team and colleagues.

» Practice Educator Standards Stage 2: Domain D (see also capability 9).

» Recognise and seek ways to promote wellbeing for team and colleagues.

» Promote up-to-date expectations about practice norms, identifying and helping resolve poor practice issues.

Values and ethics

Social workers have an obligation to conduct themselves ethically and to engage in ethical decision making, including through partnership with people who use their services. Social workers are knowledgeable about the value base of their profession, its ethical standards and relevant law.

» Demonstrate confident and critical application of professional ethical principles to decision making and practice, supporting others to do so using a legal and human rights framework.

» Model and support others to reflect on and manage the influence and impact of own values on professional practice.

» Provide guidance and support to analyse, reflect on and work with ethical dilemmas.

» Demonstrate confident application of an understanding of the benefits and limitations of partnership work, support others to do so, and promote service user and carer participation in developing service delivery.

» Promote and advance wherever possible individuals' rights to autonomy and self-determination, providing support, guidance and challenge to others.

» Demonstrate skills in the sensitive exploration of issues of privacy and information sharing in complex or risky situations, offering support and guidance to colleagues in managing such dilemmas.

Diversity

Social workers understand that diversity characterises and shapes human experience and is critical to the formation of identity. Diversity is multi-dimensional and includes race, disability, class, economic status, age, sexuality, gender and transgender, faith and belief. Social workers appreciate that, as a consequence of difference, a person's life experience may include oppression, marginalisation and alienation as well as privilege, power and acclaim, and are able to challenge appropriately.

» Inform, guide and model good practice in the application of understanding of identity and diversity to practice; identifying and taking up issues when principles of diversity are contravened in the organisation.

» Model critically reflective practice and support others to recognise and challenge discrimination, identifying and referring breaches and limitations in the ability of your own or other organisations' ability to advance equality and diversity and comply with the law.

» Demonstrate and model the effective and positive use of power and authority, whilst recognising and providing guidance to others as to how it may be used oppressively.

Rights, justice and economic wellbeing

Social workers recognise the fundamental principles of human rights and equality, and that these are protected in national and international law, conventions and policies. They ensure these principles underpin their practice. Social workers understand the importance of using and contributing to case law and applying these rights in their own practice. They understand the effects of oppression, discrimination and poverty.

» Provide guidance and challenge to others about applying the principles of social justice, social inclusion and equality to decision making.

» Demonstrate ability to interpret and use current legislation and guidance to protect and/or advance people's rights and entitlements, balancing use of different legislation to achieve the best outcomes; support colleagues (both inside and outside the organisation) to do so.

» Be able to communicate legislative issues to other professionals and agencies.

» Model best practice in applying human and civil rights, providing support to others and challenge where required.

» Support others to enable individuals to access opportunities that may enhance their economic status (eg education, work, housing, health services and welfare benefits).

» Promote access to independent advocacy, ensuring best practice and critical review, and contribute to the evaluation of independent advocacy.

Knowledge

Social workers understand psychological, social, cultural, spiritual and physical influences on people; human development throughout the life span and the legal framework for practice. They apply this knowledge in their work with individuals, families and communities. They know and use theories and methods of social work practice.

» Develop knowledge in one or more specialist areas of your practice. Expand your knowledge to inform the connections between this and other settings or areas of practice.

» Demonstrate knowledge and application of appropriate legal and policy frameworks and guidance that inform and mandate social work practice. Apply legal reasoning, using professional legal expertise and advice appropriately, recognising where scope for professional judgement exists.

» Demonstrate and apply to practice a working knowledge of human growth and development throughout the life course.

» Recognise the short- and long-term impact of psychological, socio-economic, environmental and physiological factors on people's lives, taking into account age and development, and how this informs practice.

» Recognise how systemic approaches can be used to understand the person-in-the-environment and inform your practice.

» Acknowledge the centrality of relationships for people and the key concepts of attachment, separation, loss, change and resilience.

» Understand forms of harm and their impact on people, and the implications for practice, drawing on concepts of strength, resilience, vulnerability, risk and resistance, and apply to practice.

» Demonstrate a critical knowledge of the range of theories and models for social work intervention with individuals, families, groups and communities, and the methods derived from them.

» Demonstrate a critical understanding of social welfare policy, its evolution, implementation and impact on people, social work, other professions and inter-agency working.

» Recognise the contribution, and begin to make use, of research to inform practice.

» Demonstrate a critical understanding of research methods.

» Value and take account of the expertise of service users, carers and professionals.

Critical reflection and analysis

Social workers are knowledgeable about and apply the principles of critical thinking and reasoned discernment. They identify, distinguish, evaluate and integrate multiple sources of knowledge and evidence. These include practice evidence, their own practice experience, service user and carer experience together with research-based, organisational, policy and legal knowledge. They use critical thinking augmented by creativity and curiosity.

» Routinely and efficiently apply critical reflection and analysis to increasingly complex cases.

» Draw on a wide range of evidence sources to inform decision making.

» Ensure hypotheses and options are reviewed to inform judgement and decision making.

» Start to provide professional opinion.

Intervention and skills

Social workers engage with individuals, families, groups and communities, working alongside people to assess and intervene. They enable effective relationships and are effective communicators, using appropriate skills. Using their professional judgement, they employ a range of interventions: promoting independence, providing support and protection, taking preventative action and ensuring safety whilst balancing rights and risks. They understand and take account of differentials in power, and are able to use authority appropriately. They evaluate their own practice and the outcomes for those they work with.

» Communicate skilfully and confidently in complex or high-risk situations. Model and help others to develop communication skills.

» Sustain and model engagement with people in fluctuating circumstances and capacities, including where there is hostility and risk.

» Be able to gather information quickly and effectively so as to inform judgement for interventions including in crises, and in response to challenge, or in the absence of complete information.

» Use assessment procedures discerningly so as to inform judgement.

» Maintain and expand a range of frameworks for assessment and intervention.

» Demonstrate skilled use of a range of frameworks for assessment and intervention.

» Actively support and initiate community groups and networks, including professional ones.

» Contribute to the development of the organisation's information strategy and systems.

» Model and help others with appropriate information sharing.

» Model and help others to manage changing circumstances.

» Recognise and appropriately manage the authority inherent in your position.

» Anticipate, assess and manage risk, including in more complex cases, and support others to develop risk management skills.

» Undertake assessment and planning for safeguarding in more complex cases, and help others with safeguarding skills.

Contexts and organisations

Social workers are informed about and proactively responsive to the challenges and opportunities that come with changing social contexts and constructs. They fulfil this responsibility in accordance with their professional values and ethics, both as individual professionals and as members of the organisation in which they work. They collaborate, inform and are informed by their work with others, inter-professionally and with communities.

» Keep abreast of changing contexts at local and national level, and take account of these in practice.

» Demonstrate the ability to work within your own organisation, and identify and begin to work with the relationship between the organisation, practice and wider changing contexts.

» Work to and explain the relevant legal structures in the organisation, including basic case law; know when and how to access support and appropriate legal advice and consultation.

» Explore and identify how organisational practice can support good social work practice.

» Keep abreast of changing roles in the organisation; recognise, value and engage with other specialist perspectives.

» Be confident about your role in the team, working positively with others; draw on and contribute to team working and collaborative support wherever possible.

» Take an active role in inter-professional and inter-agency work, building own network and collaborative working.

Professional leadership

The social work profession evolves through the contribution of its members in activities such as practice research, supervision, assessment of practice, teaching and management. An individual's contribution will gain influence when undertaken as part of a learning, practice-focused organisation. Learning may be facilitated with a wide range of people including social work colleagues, service users and carers, volunteers, foster carers and other professionals.

» Contribute to organisational developments.

» Play leading role in practice development in the team and help sustain a learning culture.

» Provide supervision to colleagues as organisation determines. Support others to manage and prioritise work.

» Assess and manage the work of social work students and ASYEs.

» Practice Educator Standards Stage 2: Domain B and C (see also capability 1).

Level: advanced social worker

The acronyms below indicate the capability pathways that apply to this level:

PSWE – professional social work educator,

ASWP – advanced social work practitioner,

SWM – social work manager.

Professionalism

Social workers are members of an internationally recognised profession, a title protected in UK law. Social workers demonstrate professional commitment by taking responsibility for their conduct, practice and learning, with support through supervision. As representatives of the social work profession they safeguard its reputation and are accountable to the professional regulator.

» Be able to meet the requirements of the professional regulator.

» Model the social work role; promote social work and decision making within and outside the organisation.

» Model and use critical reflective skills in management, practice or organisational supervision settings to enhance your own and others' practice.

» Model and demonstrate professionalism, ensure professional social work standards are maintained throughout your area of responsibility.

» Model and take responsibility for the positive use of workload tools; using workload data to inform the organisation's workload management and risk management approaches.

» Model and help others to maintain professional/personal boundaries and the skilled use of self in more complex situations.

» Maintain awareness of own professional limitations, knowledge gaps and conflicts of interest, actively seeking to address issues for self and others.

» Develop and maintain a network of internal and external colleagues, with whom to seek and share advice, expertise and new developments in social work.

» Foster and support an environment that promotes learning and practice development within the workplace. Foster and maintain a work environment which promotes health, safety and wellbeing of self and others.

» Identify and collaborate to resolve concerns about practice, following procedures as appropriate.

» Contribute to the development and implementation of procedures that are fit for purpose, enhance best practice and contribute to better outcomes.

Values and ethics

Social workers have an obligation to conduct themselves ethically and to engage in ethical decision making, including through partnership with people who use their services. Social workers are knowledgeable about the value base of their profession, its ethical standards and relevant law.

» Model and promote confident and critical application of professional ethics to decision-making, using a legal and human rights framework, and support others to do so.

» Model and promote a culture which encourages reflection on the influence and impact of own values on professional practice.

» Demonstrate confident management and arbitration of ethical dilemmas, providing guidance and opportunities for professional development.

» Promote and support a partnership approach to working with individuals, communities, families and carers, providing clarity and reasoning when this approach is not appropriate.

» Promote people's rights to autonomy and self-determination, supporting, challenging and guiding others as appropriate.

» Provide support and leadership when dealing with the sensitive exploration of issues of privacy and information sharing in complex or risky situations, offering support and guidance in managing such dilemmas.

Diversity

Social workers understand that diversity characterises and shapes human experience and is critical to the formation of identity. Diversity is multi-dimensional and includes race, disability, class, economic status, age, sexuality, gender and transgender, faith and belief. Social workers appreciate that, as a consequence of difference, a person's life experience may include oppression, marginalisation and alienation as well as privilege, power and acclaim, and are able to challenge appropriately.

>> Promote positive approaches to diversity and identity in your area of responsibility, providing guidance and challenge as required. Contribute to and implement policy development and decision making.

>> Create and sustain an environment where people feel supported to challenge on issues of discrimination and oppression.

>> Provide or seek out expert professional advice so that the law is complied with. Contribute to the development of relevant organisational and professional practices and procedures.

>> Model and contribute to the development of best practice in use of power and authority within your sphere of influence. Provide challenge in situations where power is used inappropriately.

Rights, justice and economic wellbeing

Social workers recognise the fundamental principles of human rights and equality, and that these are protected in national and international law, conventions and policies. They ensure these principles underpin their practice. Social workers understand the importance of using and contributing to case law and applying these rights in their own practice. They understand the effects of oppression, discrimination and poverty.

>> Monitor, review and evaluate practice to ensure application of the principles of social justice, social inclusion and equality to decision making. Contribute to policies and development opportunities to support these principles.

>> Ensure that practice is compliant with the law through the provision of or access to expert professional social work advice. Challenge situations where the interpretation of the law seems neither fair nor proportionate.

>> Model best practice, provide or seek out expert professional social work/legal advice, applying human and civil rights in complex situations where there are competing issues. Contribute to policy and practice developments to support service improvement.

>> Model and guide others on accessing appropriate opportunities that may enhance economic status. Advocate for the development of opportunities for people within your sphere of influence.

>> Offer professional SW consultation and liaison to independent advocacy. Support others to identify when independent advocacy is appropriate, and advocate for necessary resources. Provide review and challenge as necessary.

Knowledge

Social workers understand psychological, social, cultural, spiritual and physical influences on people; human development throughout the life span and the legal framework for practice. They apply this knowledge in their work with individuals, families and communities. They know and use theories and methods of social work practice.

» Encourage a culture of professional curiosity.

» Maintain a well-developed understanding of knowledge relevant to your area of practice, and a confident self-awareness of knowledge limits.

» Be able to access and make critical use of relevant knowledge from a variety of sources, and apply this knowledge in practice.

» Maintain a strong socio-cultural knowledge base (including in relation to law, human development, social, psychological and spiritual issues) and apply confidently in practice.

» Use knowledge to hypothesise and make complex judgements in uncertain and ambiguous situations, supporting and challenging others to do the same.

» Enable and challenge others to develop their knowledge base and make knowledge-informed judgements.

» Have an in-depth knowledge of adult learning and its application to practice. (PSWE)

» Have an in-depth knowledge and understanding of holistic assessment processes and theory. (PSWE)

» Have a good knowledge of team dynamics, resources and the ability to maximise people and team potential. (SWM)

» Develop and maintain expertise, informed by knowledge, in both established and emergent areas relevant to their field of practice. (ASWP)

» Support others, through consultation and shadowing, to apply knowledge to practice. (ASWP)

» Build and maintain a confident body of knowledge that informs team management practice and style. (SWM)

Critical reflection and analysis

Social workers are knowledgeable about and apply the principles of critical thinking and reasoned discernment. They identify, distinguish, evaluate and integrate multiple sources of knowledge and evidence. These include practice evidence, their own practice experience, service user and carer experience together with research-based, organisational, policy and legal knowledge. They use critical thinking augmented by creativity and curiosity.

» Maintain an environment where critical reflection and analysis is valued and supported.

» Provide critical reflection, challenge and evidence-informed decision making in complex situations. Support others in developing these capabilities, and finding their own solutions. (ASWP)

» Model good practice and reflective supervision skills.

» Develop and maintain a system within which all social workers (including you) are able to access professional supervision from appropriately experienced social workers.

» Ensure protected time is available for professional social work supervision.

» Routinely provide professional social work opinion, based on clear rationale and advanced professional knowledge.

» Support and empower others to develop the confidence and skills to provide professional opinion.

Intervention and skills

Social workers engage with individuals, families, groups and communities, working alongside people to assess and intervene. They enable effective relationships and are effective communicators, using appropriate skills. Using their professional judgement, they employ a range of interventions: promoting independence, providing support and protection, taking preventative action and ensuring safety whilst balancing rights and risks. They understand and take account of differentials in power, and are able to use authority appropriately. They evaluate their own practice and the outcomes for those they work with.

» Model and promote a culture of clear communication, supporting the development of effective communication skills in others.

» Communicate effectively in highly charged, complex or challenging circumstances to a wide range of audiences for different purposes and at different levels, including public speaking.

» Model effective engagement with a wide range of people in challenging situations, and support others to develop and maintain effective engagement, including in situations of hostility and risk.

» Promote a culture which supports empathetic compassionate relationships with other professionals, people who use services, and those who care for them.

» Be able to gather, analyse and review complex and/or contradictory information quickly and effectively, using it to reach informed professional decisions.

» Support and encourage professional decision making in others. Identify when more strategic/expert advice or decision making is needed. (SWM/ASWP)

» Maintain and provide expertise in specialist assessment and intervention, acting as a resource to others within the organisation, supporting social workers to develop. (ASWP/PSWE)

» Engage in and facilitate research and evaluation of practice. (ASWP/PSWE)

» Develop and maintain a culture that supports social/professional networks, for individuals, communities and professionals.

» Evaluate and analyse recording and the use of information systems. Use evidence gained to inform good practice and maintain a focus on positive outcomes for service users, families, carers and communities. (ASWP/SWM)

» Advise, model and support others to share information appropriately and in timely ways, including in complex situations where there are competing or contradictory rights involved.

» Manage organisational change, supporting others to do so in ways which maintain a focus on positive outcomes for people who use services, families, carers and communities. Model the appropriate use of authority across a range of situations, supporting others to understand and work with the authority inherent in their positions.

» Promote use of evidence and theory to support practice in complex and changing circumstances. (ASWP/PSWE)

» Support effective interventions in the lives of people experiencing complex and challenging change. (ASWP/SWM)

» Model effective assessment and management of risk in complex situations, across a range of situations, including positive risk-taking approaches.

» Support and enable staff to have conversations with service users and others to manage risk, decision making themselves where possible.

» Be able to work with and contain the anxiety of others in relation to risk, ensuring that there is a positive balance between perceived risk and protection from harm when necessary. (ASWP/SWM)

» Ensure risk assessment and management reflect current best practice and research developments, including supporting service users and others to manage their own risks where possible. (PSWE/ASWP)

Contexts and organisations

Social workers are informed about and proactively responsive to the challenges and opportunities that come with changing social contexts and constructs. They fulfil this responsibility in accordance with their professional values and ethics, both as individual professionals and as members of the organisation in which they work. They collaborate, inform and are informed by their work with others, inter-professionally and with communities.

» Maintain an awareness of changes in national and local contexts and their impact on practice, and communicate this effectively within and outside of the organisation. Positively influence developments that affect social work practice.

» Provide professional leadership and facilitate collaboration within a multi-agency context as appropriate.

» Maintain a sophisticated knowledge of the law relevant to your area of practice, advise others and facilitate access to and dissemination of more specialist advice where necessary.

» Contribute to and provide professional leadership of organisational change and development, including the identification of gaps in service.

» Influence organisational development, proactively using feedback from your areas of responsibility.

» Address and oversee performance management issues that arise, supporting people to positively resolve difficulties where possible, taking action with HR/the regulator where necessary.

» Promote positive working relationships in and across teams, using strategies for collaboration and contribute to a supportive organisational culture.

» Develop and contribute to liaison across agencies at a local and regional level, maintain a collaborative working approach, resolving dilemmas actively where necessary.

Professional leadership

The social work profession evolves through the contribution of its members in activities such as practice research, supervision, assessment of practice, teaching and management. An individual's contribution will gain influence when undertaken as part of a learning, practice-focused organisation. Learning may be facilitated with a wide range of people including social work colleagues, service users and carers, volunteers, foster carers and other professionals.

» Promote and develop professional leadership within your area of responsibility.

» Promote a culture of professional curiosity embracing research within your area of responsibility, encouraging the exploration of different cultures, concepts and ideas.

» Contribute to the identification, planning and meeting of staff development needs within the workplace, informed by the PCF.

» Take responsibility for ensuring individual and workplace practice is informed by and informs research and current professional knowledge.

» Promote, articulate and support a positive social work identity.

» Have regard to the requirements of the Standards for Employers of Social Workers.

» Ensure systems are in place to provide high quality professional and line management supervision (as appropriate to the role), using critical reflection and a range of other supervisory techniques.

» Assure high quality professional supervision for all (including those providing supervision) within your area of responsibility.

» Provide professional, reflective supervision and support to others. (ASWP)

» Be able to identify and develop potential within other staff.

» Understand concepts of holistic assessment of professional capability, and be able to apply to appraisal processes/performance reviews of social workers within your area of responsibility.

Level: strategic

The following acronyms indicate the capability pathways that apply to this level:

PSWE – professional social work educator,

PSW – principal social worker,

SSWE – strategic social work educator,

ASWP – advanced social work practitioner,

SWM – social work manager,

SSWM – strategic social work manager.

Values and ethics

Social workers have an obligation to conduct themselves ethically and to engage in ethical decision making, including through partnership with people who use their services. Social workers are knowledgeable about the value base of their profession, its ethical standards and relevant law.

» Provide leadership in the critical application of professional ethics to strategic decision making, using a legal and human rights framework.

» Develop and promote an organisational culture which encourages reflection on the influence and impact of own or agency values on organisational culture and practice.

» Demonstrate confident leadership for the organisation in taking account of and arbitrating in complex ethical situations.

» Lead effective partnership working within and outside of the organisation, creating a culture that promotes meaningful participation of individuals, communities, families and carers. Ensure that the outcomes that service users and carers experience are the focus for review.

» Promote a culture where individuals and communities can exercise their rights to autonomy and self-determination; ensuring this is balanced against the responsibility not to harm others or be harmed themselves.

» Lead on ensuring that policies and strategies concerning information sharing and privacy are informed by current legal and professional requirements concerning safeguarding, information sharing, confidentiality and data protection.

» Ensure the organisation is aware of, and responds to changes in legislation and guidance.

Diversity

Social workers understand that diversity characterises and shapes human experience and is critical to the formation of identity. Diversity is multi-dimensional and includes race, disability, class, economic status, age, sexuality, gender and transgender, faith and belief. Social workers appreciate that, as a consequence of difference, a person's life experience may include oppression, marginalisation and alienation as well as privilege, power and acclaim, and are able to challenge appropriately.

» Lead and be accountable for strategic approaches to diversity and identity creating and embedding equality and diversity within the organisation.

» Create and sustain an organisational environment where people feel supported to challenge on issues of discrimination and oppression.

» Lead on ensuring that policies, practice and strategies concerning discrimination and oppression reflect the law and current best practice.

» Lead and model at the strategic level appropriate and effective use of power and authority. Provide challenge in situations where power is used inappropriately.

Rights, justice and economic wellbeing

Social workers recognise the fundamental principles of human rights and equality, and that these are protected in national and international law, conventions and policies. They ensure these principles underpin their practice. Social workers understand the importance of using and contributing to case law and applying these rights in their own practice. They understand the effects of oppression, discrimination and poverty.

» Take responsibility for developing and sustaining a culture where the principles of social justice, social inclusion and equality are applied to strategic decision making.

» Take strategic responsibility for ensuring that the service is compliant with the law, and secure the provision of expert advice, making judicious use of such advice. Create and sustain environments where people are enabled to provide effective challenge and ensure human rights are upheld.

» Secure expert advice in complex human and civil rights situations to ensure an appropriate and proportionate response by the organisation. Promote and contribute to policy and practice developments to support service improvement.

» Develop strategies (including regarding resources and commissioning) to promote social inclusion and access to opportunities which may enhance people's economic status.

» Monitor and evaluate their effectiveness and impact, leading and informing new approaches. Take action to address and alleviate emerging issues, working proactively with partner organisations to achieve positive outcomes. (SSWM/ PSW)

» Create an environment that promotes partnership working with independent advocates. Ensure resources are available to support access to independent advocacy, in line with statutory duties and local need.

Knowledge

Social workers understand psychological, social, cultural, spiritual and physical influences on people; human development throughout the life span and the legal framework for practice. They apply this knowledge in their work with individuals, families and communities. They know and use theories and methods of social work practice.

» Encourage a culture of professional curiosity.

» Maintain a well-developed understanding of knowledge relevant to your area of organisational practice, and a confident self-awareness of knowledge limits.

» Access and make critical use of relevant knowledge from a variety of sources, and apply this knowledge in strategic settings.

» Continue to maintain and use a strong socio-cultural knowledge base (including in relation to law, human development, social, psychological and spiritual issues) to inform strategic thinking and decision making.

» Be able to apply knowledge to hypothesise and make complex decisions in strategic situations.

» Ensure the organisation structure accommodates, through a range of approaches, appropriate resourcing for the development of and critical engagement with knowledge debates.

» Actively challenge structures and processes which inhibit knowledge development and debate.

» Ensure access to knowledge resources and relevant practice debates.

» Lead and promote the incorporation of adult learning into workforce development. Use knowledge of adult learning theories to lead the development of a learning organisation. (SSWE)

» Identify and address knowledge gaps across the organisation. (SSWE)

» Commission knowledge development of holistic assessment. (SSWE)

» Ensure social work workforce strategies address and incorporate supporting the development of practice knowledge. (SSWE)

» Have a good knowledge of organisational dynamics, resources and the ability to maximise team and organisational potential. (SSWM)

» Maintain a high level of expertise, informed by knowledge in both established and emergent areas relevant to their field of practice. (PSW)

» Provide consultation that is knowledge informed to professional/strategic decision making. (PSW/SSWM)

» Maintain and model a confident body of knowledge that informs management practice and style. (SSWM)

Critical reflection and analysis

Social workers are knowledgeable about and apply the principles of critical thinking and reasoned discernment. They identify, distinguish, evaluate and integrate multiple sources of knowledge and evidence. These include practice evidence, their own practice experience, service user and carer experience together with research-based, organisational, policy and legal knowledge. They use critical thinking augmented by creativity and curiosity.

» Take responsibility for the creation and maintenance of an organisational environment within which critical reflection and analysis take place and are valued and supported.

» Promote and provide critical reflection, challenge and evidence-informed decision making in complex situations. Support others in developing these capabilities, and finding their own solutions. (PSW)

» Model good practice and reflective supervision skills.

» Take strategic responsibility for the development of a system of critical analysis and reflective professional supervision at all levels within the organisation, ensuring this is appropriately resourced, in line with the Standards for Employers. (SSWM/PSW)

» Routinely provide professional social work opinion within a strategic context.

» Using evidence and practice knowledge, be the voice of professional social work opinion within strategic decision making. (PSW)

» Be responsible for ensuring that the value of social work professional knowledge and opinion influences good practice, service delivery and organisational strategy. (PSW)

» Champion the development of empowered professional social work decision makers throughout the organisation.

Intervention and skills

Social workers engage with individuals, families, groups and communities, working alongside people to assess and intervene. They enable effective relationships and are effective communicators, using appropriate skills. Using their professional judgement, they employ a range of interventions: promoting independence, providing support and protection, taking preventative action and ensuring safety whilst balancing rights and risks. They understand and take account of differentials in power, and are able to use authority appropriately. They evaluate their own practice and the outcomes for those they work with.

» Model effective communication skills within a strategic context, creating the opportunity/environment where effective communication is promoted within the organisation.

» Communicate in an effective and competent manner in highly charged, complex or challenging circumstances in strategic settings, inside and outside the organisation.

» Ensure strategic communication is informed by current direct practice experience. (PSW)

» Provide effective strategic leadership, support and model engagement in the most challenging of circumstances, including with partner agencies, stakeholders and other professionals.

» Create an ethos in the organisation where social workers are supported to engage positively with people in challenging circumstances.

» Maintain empathetic compassionate relationships with strategic leads, other professionals, people who use services and those who care for them.

» Be able to gather complex and/or contradictory information, analyse it from different perspectives as a strategic leader and professional social worker, and use it to inform organisational and professional decision making.

» Support and enable others to use their own experience and expertise to analyse information and make informed professional decisions.

» Maintain and use expert assessment and intervention skills in complex practice situations, and support others to do so. Engage in and facilitate research and evaluation of practice. (PSW)

» Develop a culture that supports and encourages engagement in research, as well as development and maintenance of expert intervention skills. (PSW/SSWE)

» Create and maintain a culture of support for engagement with networks both within and outside of the organisation. Develop strategic engagement with a range of stakeholder groups.

» Strategically understand the interface between information systems and practice, and ensure systems support delivery of positive outcomes for people who use services, families, carers and communities. (PSW)

» Take action to ensure information systems continue to be fit for practice.

» Have responsibility for advising and contributing to the organisation's information governance system, and ensure implementation is congruent with social work practice and legal requirements.

» Lead change within and across organisations, ensuring that strategic decisions are informed by social work knowledge and practice, and the need to develop positive outcomes for service users, carers and communities.

» Model the appropriate use of authority across a range of complex and challenging situations, ensuring that systems are in place to support the appropriate use of professional authority by social workers within the organisation.

» Lead the development and use of evidence-informed risk assessment, which support both responsiveness and positive risk taking to improve outcomes for people who use services, families, carers and communities. (PSW)

» Be able to work with and contain the anxiety of other people in complex and highly charged situations, ensuring that there is a proportionate response between perceived risk and protection from harm when necessary. (PSW/SSWM)

» Lead and develop an organisational culture which is responsive to developing best practice and research around risk assessment and management, at all levels of the organisation. (PSW/SSWM)

» Develop service user outcome focused evaluation of their experience of the social work interventions, such as safeguarding, and embed any learning into practice. (PSW/SSWM)

Contexts and organisations

Social workers are informed about and proactively responsive to the challenges and opportunities that come with changing social contexts and constructs. They fulfil this responsibility in accordance with their professional values and ethics, both as individual professionals and as members of the organisation in which they work. They collaborate, inform and are informed by their work with others, inter-professionally and with communities.

» Anticipate and provide strategic leadership for social workers and others, engaging locally, regionally and nationally, to positively influence developments that affect social work.

» Initiate and facilitate effective multi-agency partnership working, to drive improvements in performance and outcomes for people who use services, families, carers and communities.

» Maintain a sophisticated knowledge of the law relevant to your area of responsibility, using it to support strategic decision making. Advise others and seek out specialist advice where necessary. Ensure social workers have access to legal advice and information where needed.

» Initiate, facilitate and enable organisational development at a local, regional and national level, providing professional leadership as needed.

» Lead the positive use of mechanisms for feedback about social work to inform organisational development.

» Ensure that a social work perspective informs organisational decision making. (PSW)

» Develop and maintain a strategic plan to oversee performance management themes that arise, supporting positive resolutions and taking action with HR/the regulator where necessary.

» Promote positive working relationships across the organisation, using strategies to support collaboration and a supportive organisational culture.

» Initiate, facilitate and lead liaison across agencies at a local, regional and national level, maintain a collaborative working approach, resolving intractable dilemmas where necessary.

Professional leadership

The social work profession evolves through the contribution of its members in activities such as practice research, supervision, assessment of practice, teaching and management. An individual's contribution will gain influence when undertaken as part of a learning, practice-focused organisation. Learning may be facilitated with a wide range of people including social work colleagues, service users and carers, volunteers, foster carers and other professionals.

» Model professional social work leadership, and provide opportunities to support others' development.

» Lead a culture of professional curiosity within the organisation, embracing research and encouraging the exploration of different cultures, concepts and ideas.

» Ensure there is appropriate provision to identify, plan for and meet staff development needs within the organisation so that workforce planning and appraisal are informed by the PCF.

» Create opportunities and systems for current practice to inform and be informed by research and current professional knowledge.

» Lead, articulate and promote a positive social work identity which actively seeks and respects the contributions and views of all.

» Drive improvement in line with the Standards for Employers of Social Workers.

» Create and promote a culture of high quality supervision which covers practice, organisational and management issues (as appropriate to the role) promoting critical reflection throughout the organisation. Ensure systems are in place to monitor effectiveness.

» Ensure effective, sufficient and appropriate supervision is embedded across the organisation and that a strategy is in place to ensure that professional supervisors are trained and skilled in a range of approaches.

» Lead a culture of talent identification and development.

» Understand concepts of holistic assessment of professional capability, and be able to apply to appraisal processes/performance reviews of social workers within your area of responsibility.

Professionalism

Social workers are members of an internationally recognised profession, a title protected in UK law. Social workers demonstrate professional commitment by taking responsibility for their conduct, practice and learning, with support through supervision. As representatives of the social work profession they safeguard its reputation and are accountable to the professional regulator.

» Be able to meet the requirements of the professional regulator.

» Model the social work role at a senior level, taking a strategic approach to representing and promoting the profession within and outside of the organisation.

» Model and use critical reflective skills in management, practice or organisational supervision settings to enhance your own, others' and the organisation's strategic outcomes.

» Model and demonstrate professionalism, ensuring professional social work standards are promoted and enhanced throughout the organisation.

» Identify and quantify the social work and other resources required to support the work of the organisation. Take responsibility for the implementation and evaluation of workload tools. Ensure the organisation's workload is actively monitored and evaluated, taking action to promote positive solutions.

» Model the sophisticated use of self, and professional/personal boundaries in a range of complex situations, and ensure policies and procedures recognise or reflect this approach.

» Maintain awareness of own professional limitations, knowledge gaps and conflicts of interest and actively seek to address issues for self and others.

» Maintain a professional and strategic network of internal and external colleagues, with whom to seek and share advice, expertise and new developments in social work.

» Create and sustain an environment that promotes learning and practice development, facilitating research within the organisation and with strategic partners.

» Create and sustain a work environment that promotes health, safety and wellbeing of self and others across the organisation.

» Create and maintain a culture where concerns about practice are effectively dealt with, including reporting to the regulator as appropriate.

» Take responsibility to ensure that organisational procedures are relevant, reflect effective practice and contribute to better outcomes.

Appendix 2: Knowledge and Skills Statements

Knowledge and Skills Statement – child and family social work

A child and family social worker should be able to do the following:

1) Relationships and effective direct work

Build effective relationships with children, young people and families, which form the bedrock of all support and child protection responses. Be both authoritative and empathic and work in partnership with children, families and professionals, enabling full participation in assessment, planning, review and decision making. Ensure child protection is always privileged.

Provide support based on best evidence, which is tailored to meet individual child and family needs, and which addresses relevant and significant risks. Secure access to services, negotiating and challenging other professionals and organisations to provide the help required. Ensure children and families, including children in public care, receive the support to which they are entitled.

Support children and families in transition, including children and young people moving to and between placements, those returning home, those being adopted or moving through to independence. Help children to separate from, and sustain, multiple relationships recognising the impact of loss and change.

2) Communication

Communicate clearly and sensitively with children of different ages and abilities, their families and in a range of settings and circumstances. Use methods based on best evidence. Create immediate rapport with people not previously known which facilitates engagement and motivation to participate in child protection enquiries, assessments and services.

Act respectfully even when people are angry, hostile and resistant to change. Manage tensions between parents, carers and family members, in ways that show persistence, determination and professional confidence.

Listen to the views, wishes and feelings of children and families and help parents and carers understand the ways in which their children communicate through their behaviour. Help them to understand how they might communicate more effectively with their children.

Promote speech, language and communication support, identifying those children and adults who are experiencing difficulties expressing themselves. Produce written case notes and reports, which are well argued, focused, and jargon free. Present a clear analysis and a sound rationale for actions as well as any conclusions reached, so that all parties are well informed.

3) Child development

Observe and talk to children in their environment including at home, at school, with parents, carers, friends and peers to help understand the physical and emotional world in which the child lives, including the quality of child and parent/carer interaction and other key relationships. Establish the pattern of development for the child, promote optimal child development and be alert to signs that may indicate that the child is not meeting key developmental milestones, has been harmed or is at risk of harm.

Take account of typical age-related physical, cognitive, social, emotional and behavioural development over time, accepting that normative developmental tasks are different for each child depending on the interaction for that child between health, environmental and genetic factors. Assess the influence of cultural and social factors on child development, the effect of different parenting styles, and the effect of loss, change and uncertainty in the development of resilience.

Explore the extent to which behavioural and emotional development may also be a result of communication difficulties, ill health or disability, adjusting practice to take account of these differences. Seek further advice from relevant professionals to fully understand a child's development and behaviour.

4) Adult mental ill health, substance misuse, domestic abuse, physical ill health and disability

Identify the impact of adult mental ill health, substance misuse, domestic abuse, physical ill health and disability on family functioning and social circumstances and in particular the effect on children, including those who are young carers. Access the help and assistance of other professionals in the identification and prevention of adult social need and risk, including mental health and learning disability assessment.

Coordinate emergency and routine services and synthesise multi-disciplinary judgements as part of ongoing social work assessment. Use a range of strategies to help families facing these difficulties.

Identify concerning adult behaviours that may indicate risk or increasing risk to children. Assess the likely impact on, and inter-relationship between, parenting and child development. Recognise and act upon escalating social needs and risks, helping to ensure that vulnerable adults are safeguarded and that a child is protected and their best interests always prioritised.

5) Abuse and neglect of children

Exchange information with partner agencies about children and adults where there is concern about the safety and welfare of children. Triangulate evidence to ensure robust conclusions are drawn. Recognise harm and the risk indicators of different forms of harm to children relating to sexual, physical, emotional abuse and neglect. Take into account the long-term effects of cumulative harm, particularly in relation to early indicators of neglect.

Consider the possibility of child sexual exploitation, grooming (online and offline), female genital mutilation and enforced marriage and the range of adult behaviours which pose a risk to children, recognising too the potential for children to be perpetrators of abuse.

Lead the investigation of allegations of significant harm to children in consultation with other professionals and practice supervisors. Draw one's own conclusions about the likelihood of, for example, sexual abuse or non-accidental injury having occurred and the extent to which any injury is consistent with the explanation offered. Commission a second professional opinion and take legal advice where necessary.

6) Child and family assessment

Carry out in-depth and ongoing family assessment of social need and risk to children, with particular emphasis on parental capacity and capability to change. Use professional curiosity and authority while maintaining a position of partnership, involving all key family members, including fathers. Acknowledge any conflict between parental and children's interests, prioritising the protection of children as set out in legislation.

Use child observation skills, genograms, ecomaps, chronologies and other evidence based tools ensuring active child and family participation in the process. Incorporate the contributions that other professional disciplines make to social work assessments.

Hold an empathic position about difficult social circumstances experienced by children and families, taking account of the relationship between poverty and social deprivation, and the effect of stress on family functioning, providing help and support. Take into account individual child and family history and how this might affect the ability of adults and children to engage with services. Recognise and address behaviour that may indicate resistance to change, ambivalent or selective cooperation with services, and recognise when there is a need for immediate action, and what other steps can be taken to protect children.

7) Analysis, decision-making, planning and review

Establish the seriousness that different risks present and any harm already suffered by a child, balanced with family strengths and potential solutions. Set out the best options for resolving difficulties facing the family and each child, considering the risk of future harm and its consequences and the likelihood of successful change.

Prioritise children's need for emotional warmth, stability and sense of belonging, particularly those in public care, as well as identity development, health and education, ensuring active participation and positive engagement of the child and family. Test multiple hypotheses about what is happening in families and to children, using evidence and professional judgement to reach timely conclusions. Challenge any prevailing professional conclusions in the light of new evidence or practice reflection.

Make realistic, child centred, plans within a review timeline, which will manage and reduce identified risks and meet the needs of the child. Ensure sufficient multi-disciplinary input into the process at all stages. Apply twin and triple track planning to minimise chances of drift or delay, being alert to the effectiveness or otherwise of current support plans.

8) The law and the family and youth justice systems

Navigate the family and youth justice systems in England using legal powers and duties to support families, to protect children and to look after children in the public care system, including the regulatory frameworks that support the full range of permanence options. Participate in decisions about whether to make an application to the family court, the order to be applied for, and the preparation and presentation of evidence.

Seek advice and second opinion as required in relation to the wide range of legal issues which frequently face children and families involved with statutory services including immigration, housing, welfare benefits, mental health and learning disability assessment, education and support for children with learning difficulties.

Use the law, regulatory and statutory guidance to inform practice decisions. Take into account the complex relationship between professional ethics, the application of the law and the impact of social policy on both.

9) The role of supervision

Recognise one's own professional limitations and how and when to seek advice from a range of sources, including practice supervisors, senior practice leaders and other clinical practitioners from a range of disciplines such as psychiatry, paediatrics and psychology. Discuss, debate, reflect upon and test hypotheses about what is happening within families, and with children.

Explore the potential for bias in decision-making and resolve tensions emerging from, for example, ethical dilemmas, conflicting information or differing professional positions. Identify which methods will be of help for a specific child or family and the limitations of different approaches. Make use of the best evidence from research to inform the complex judgements and decisions needed to support families and protect children.

Reflect on the emotional experience of working relationships with parents, carers and children, and consciously identify where personal triggers are affecting the quality of analysis or help. Identify strategies to build professional resilience and management of self.

10) Organisational context

Operate successfully in a wide range of organisational contexts complying with the checks and balances within local and national systems which are a condition of employment. Maintain personal and professional credibility through effective working relationships with peers, managers and leaders both within the profession, throughout multi-agency partnerships and public bodies, including the family courts.

Act in ways that protect the reputation of the employer organisation and the social work profession, whilst always privileging the best interests of children. Manage the specific set of organisational tasks relating to lead responsibility for children with the support of an appropriately qualified supervisor and use of the multi-agency support network.

Contribute to the organisation's role as corporate parent to children in public care, encouraging and advocating for organisational focus, resource and support so that children and young people can thrive and enjoy their childhood and move into independence with confidence in and ambition for their futures.

Knowledge and Skills Statement – for social workers in adult services

1. Statement overview

This statement sets out what a social worker working with adults should know and be able to do by the end of their Assessed and Supported Year in Employment (ASYE). The statement incorporates the experiences and perspectives of front line social workers, their managers, organisations and educators. It has been developed by the Chief Social Worker for adults in partnership with key stakeholders, including The College of Social Work, the British Association of Social Workers, Skills for Care, Social Care Institute for Excellence, educators and principal social workers. The statement relates to all social workers working with adults who contribute to delivering statutory health and wellbeing outcomes for people and their carers, regardless of the sector in which they are employed and provides a national benchmark for social workers, employers and the public.

It sets out a national framework for the assessment of newly qualified social workers at the end of their first year in practice, including provision for independent validation and quality assurance of the assessment process. It should be used by social workers and their employers to build a wider framework for induction, supervision and the continuing professional development of social workers and the social work profession. Social work is an international profession and is practiced in many different settings and specialisms. This statement builds on the global definition for social work, the Health and Care Professions Council (HCPC) Standards of Proficiency for social workers and the generic Professional Capabilities Framework, which sets the professional standards for social workers in England. It also builds on key policy documents developed by The College of Social Work, namely:

» The Role and Functions of Social Workers in England;

» The Business Case for Social Work with Adults; and

» The Role of Social Workers in Adult Mental Health Services.

This statement is designed to strengthen and enhance the Professional Capabilities Framework by setting out what we expect of newly qualified social workers working in adult social care and importantly, reinforcing the support and arrangements employers need to provide as set out in the Standards for Employers.

Although not mandatory, all social workers should be able to demonstrate knowledge of all aspects of the statement and development in those aspects which are relevant to the service setting. The statement represents the first step on a social worker's career pathway, starting from the end of their final placement in their social work degree, to the end of their first year in practice and through the PCF levels thereafter.

The Department will work with The College of Social Work and the sector to map in more detail the relationship between the requirements set out in this Statement, the Knowledge and Skills Statement for Child and Family Social Work and the relevant capabilities in the Professional Capabilities Framework.

2. The role of social workers working with adults

The Care Act 2014 puts the principle of individual wellbeing and professional practice of the individual social worker at the heart of adult social care and signals a move away from care management as the overriding approach to working with adults.

Social workers need to apply a wide range of knowledge and skills to understand and build relationships, and work directly with individuals, their families and carers to enable and empower them to achieve best outcomes. This should include undertaking assessments, planning care and support and making the best use of available resources to enable people to have better lives. Social workers should enable people to experience personalised, integrated care and support them to maintain their independence and wellbeing, cope with change, attain the outcomes they want and need, understand and manage risk, and participate in the life of their communities. Social work should focus on the links between the individual, their health and well being and their need for relationships and connection with their families, community and wider society. Social workers in adult social care must understand and be able to explain the role of social work as part of the system of health and welfare support to individuals and families. They must understand the impact of poverty, inequality and diversity on social and economic opportunities and how these relate to people's health and wellbeing as well as the functioning of their families, particularly in connection with child protection, adult safeguarding and also empowering individuals who may lack mental capacity.

3. Person-centred practice

Social workers should enable people to access the advice, support and services to which they are entitled. They should coordinate and facilitate a wide range of practical and emotional support, and discharge legal duties to complement people's own resources and networks, so that all individuals (no matter their background, health status or mental capacity), carers and families can exercise choice and control, (supporting individuals to make their own decisions, especially where they may lack capacity) and meet their needs and aspirations in personalised, creative and often novel ways. They should work co-productively and innovatively with people, local communities, other professionals, agencies and services to promote self-determination, community capacity, personal and family reliance, cohesion, earlier intervention and active citizenship. Social workers should also engage with and enable access to advocacy for people who may require help to secure the support and care they need due to physical or mental ill-health, sensory or communication impairment, learning disability, mental incapacity, frailty or a combination of these conditions and their physical, psychological and social consequences.

4. Safeguarding

Social workers must be able to recognise the risk indicators of different forms of abuse and neglect and their impact on individuals, their families or their support networks and should prioritise the protection of children and adults in vulnerable situations whenever necessary. This includes working with those who self-neglect.

Social workers who work with adults must take an outcomes-focused, person-centred approach to safeguarding practice, recognising that people are experts in their own lives and working alongside them to identify person centred solutions to risk and harm. In situations where there is abuse or neglect or clear risk of those, social workers must work in a way that enhances involvement, choice and control as part of improving quality of life, wellbeing and safety.

Social workers should take the lead in managing positive interventions that prevent deterioration in health and wellbeing; safeguard people (who may or may not be socially excluded) at risk of abuse or neglect, or who are subject to discrimination, and to take necessary action where someone poses a risk to themselves, their children or other people. Social workers who work with adults must be able to recognise and take appropriate action where they come across situations where a child or young person may be at risk.

Social workers should understand and apply in practice personalised approaches to safeguarding adults that maximise the adult's opportunity to determine and realise their desired outcomes and to safeguard themselves effectively, with support where necessary.

5 .Mental capacity

Social workers must have a thorough knowledge and understanding of the Mental Capacity Act (MCA) and Code of Practice and be able to apply these in practice. They should always begin from the presumption that individuals have capacity to make the decision in question.

Social workers should understand how to make a capacity assessment, the decision and time specific nature of capacity and hence the need to reassess capacity appropriately. They should know when and how to refer to a Best Interest Assessor.

Social workers must understand their responsibilities for people who are assessed as lacking capacity at a particular time and must ensure that they are supported to be involved in decisions about themselves and their care as far as is possible. Where they are unable to be involved in the decision-making process decisions should be taken in their best interests following consultation with all appropriate parties, including families and carers. Social workers must seek to ensure that an individual's care plan is the least restrictive possible to achieve the intended outcomes.

Social workers have a key leadership role in modelling to other professionals the proper application of the MCA. Key to this is the understanding that the MCA exists to empower those who lack capacity as much as it exists to protect them. Social workers must model and lead a change of approach, away from that where the default setting is 'safety first', towards a person-centred culture where individual choice is encouraged and where the right of all individuals to express their own lifestyle choices is recognised and valued.

In working with those where there is no concern over capacity, social workers should take all practicable steps to empower people to make their own decisions, recognising that people are experts in their own lives and working alongside them to identify person-centred solutions to risk and harm, recognising the individual's right to make 'unwise' decisions.

6. Effective assessments and outcome based support planning

In undertaking assessments, social workers must be able to recognise the expertise of the diverse people with whom they work and their carers and apply this to develop personalised assessment and care plans that enable the individual to determine and achieve the outcomes they want for themselves. The social worker must ensure the individual's views, wishes and feelings (including those who may lack mental capacity) are included as part of their full participation in decision making, balancing this with the wellbeing of their carers. Social workers should demonstrate a good understanding of personalisation, the social model of disability and of human development throughout life and demonstrate a holistic approach to the identification of needs, circumstances, rights, strengths and risks. In particular, social workers need to understand the impact of trauma, loss and abuse, physical disability, physical ill health, learning disability, mental ill health, mental capacity, substance misuse, domestic abuse, aging and end of life issues on physical, cognitive, emotional and social development both for the individual and for the functioning of the family. They should recognise the roles and needs of informal or family carers and use holistic, systemic approaches to supporting individuals and carers. They should develop and maintain knowledge and good partnerships with local community resources in order to work effectively with individuals in connecting them with appropriate resources and support.

7. Direct work with individuals and families

Social workers need to be able to work directly with individuals and their families through the professional use of self, using interpersonal skills and emotional intelligence to create relationships based on openness, transparency and empathy. They should know how to build purposeful, effective relationships underpinned by reciprocity. They should be able to communicate clearly, sensitively and effectively, applying a range of best evidence-based methods of written, oral and non-verbal communication and adapt these methods to match the person's age, comprehension and culture. Social workers should be capable of communicating effectively with people with specific communication needs, including those with learning disabilities, dementia, people who lack mental capacity and people with sensory impairment. They should do this in ways that are engaging, respectful, motivating and effective, even when dealing with conflict – whether perceived or actual – anger and resistance to change. Social workers should have a high level of skill in applying evidence-based, effective social work approaches to help service users and families handle change, especially where individuals and families are in transition, including young people moving to adulthood, supporting them to move to different living arrangements and understanding the impact of loss and change.

8. Supervision, critical reflection and analysis

Social workers must have access to regular, good quality supervision and understand its importance in providing advice and support. They should know how and when to seek advice from a range of sources including named supervisors, senior social workers and other professionals. They should be able to make effective use of opportunities to discuss, reflect upon and test multiple hypotheses, the role of intuition and logic in decision making, the difference between opinion and fact, the role of evidence, how to address common bias in situations of uncertainty and the reasoning of any conclusions reached and recommendations made, particularly in relation to mental capacity, mental health and safeguarding situations.

Social workers should have a critical understanding of the difference between theory, research, evidence and expertise and the role of professional judgement. They should use practice evidence and research to inform the complex judgements and decisions needed to support, empower and protect their service users. They should apply imagination, creativity and curiosity to working in partnership with individuals and their carers, acknowledging the centrality of people's own expertise about their experience and needs.

9. Organisational context

Social workers working with adults should be able confidently to fulfil their statutory responsibilities, work within their organisation's remit and contribute to its development. They must understand and work effectively within financial and legal frameworks, obligations, structures and culture, in particular Human Rights and Equalities legislation, the Care Act, Mental Capacity Act, Mental Health Act and accompanying guidance and codes of practice. They must be able to operate successfully in their organisational context, demonstrating effective time management, caseload management and be capable of reconciling competing demands and embrace information, data and technology appropriate to their role. They should have access to regular quality supervision to support their professional resilience and emotional and physical wellbeing. Social workers should work effectively and confidently with fellow professionals in inter-agency, multi-disciplinary and inter-professional groups and demonstrate effective partnership working particularly in the context of health and social care integration and at the interface between health, children and adult social care and the third sector.

10. Professional ethics and leadership

Social workers should be able to explain their role to stakeholders, particularly health and community partners, and challenge partners constructively to effect multi-agency working. They should contribute to developing awareness of personalisation and outcome-based approaches to improving people's lives. Social workers should be able to demonstrate the principles of social work through professional judgement, decision making and actions within a framework of professional accountability. They should be able to work collaboratively to manage effectively the sometimes competing interests of service users, their families and their carers ensuring that the needs of all parties are appropriately balanced, but that where children are involved, the children's interests are always paramount. They should be able to acknowledge the inherent tensions where there is a dual role of care and control; be able to meet eligible needs within limited resources and manage the emotions and expectations of service users and carers. They should be able to identify potential deprivations of liberty and understand the process for assessing and authorising these in individuals' best interests. They should feed back the views and experiences of clients and their colleagues to contribute to the continued improvement of services, policies and procedures within the organisation. They must be able to recognise and address poor practice and systemic failings which put people at risk, whether in their own organisation or the organisations and institutions with which they are working, making appropriate use of whistle-blowing procedures.

11. Level of capability: social worker working in an adult setting at the end of their first year in employment

By the end of the Assessed and Supported Year in Employment social workers working in an adult setting should have consistently demonstrated proficiency in a wide range of tasks and roles. For example, they will be able to complete assessments of need independently, which start from a perspective of the service users' desired outcomes and have become more effective in their interventions; deal with more complex situations; develop respectful and situation appropriate professional relationships, thus building their own confidence; and earn the confidence and respect of others. They will have a good understanding of risk assessment and positive risk taking and be able to apply this to practice to ensure person centred planning approaches and individual rights are upheld. They will have developed confidence in working within multidisciplinary settings, understanding their roles and be able to maintain and express a clear social work perspective. They will have experience and skills in relation to a particular setting and user group, be able to understand and work within the legal frameworks relevant to adult settings, in particular, the Mental Capacity Act, Mental Health Act and the Care Act, and fully operate within the organisational context, policies and procedures. They will be able to confidently undertake mental capacity assessments in routine situations; to identify and work proactively and in partnership around safeguarding issues and have demonstrated the ability to work effectively in more complex situations. They will seek support in supervision appropriately, whilst starting to exercise initiative and evaluate their own practice. For example, they should take responsibility for cases allocated to them, be proactive in identifying issues and recommending actions, but be aware of when to seek further advice and support in more complex situations. They will be able to reflect on their practice and continue to identify learning and development to further consolidate their knowledge and skills. They will have developed some resilience and leadership skills and be able to demonstrate sound professional judgment and will know how to argue for appropriate resource allocation to meet assessed needs.

12. The National Framework for the Assessment of Social Workers at the end of their Assessed and Supported Year in Employment

We will introduce a national system of quality assurance so that the profession can have confidence that employers' judgements are consistent across the country. This national scheme will have two parts: standardised arrangements for assessment and moderation led by Skills for Care; and a national system for validating the implementation of these arrangements across the country, led by The College of Social Work. These arrangements will build on existing processes and are intended to produce improved national consistency in standards and assessment of the Assessed and Supported Year in Employment for social workers in adult services.

To ensure national consistency in the assessment of social workers at the end of their first year of practice:

1. The Assessed and Supported Year in Employment assessor must be a registered social worker.

2. The assessment must include:

    a) three formal direct observations of practice undertaken by a registered social worker (at least two of these to be completed by the assessor);

    b) at least three pieces of feedback over the course of the year from people who need care and support, or from their carers;

    c) at least three pieces of feedback over the course of the year from other professionals;

    d) the assessment of a written piece of work demonstrating the ability of the employee to reflect on and learn from practice: it should show how the employee has used critical reflection on their practice to improve their professional skills and demonstrate reasoned judgment relating to a practice decision;

    e) the assessment of at least three examples of written reports and records, including a report written for an external decision making processes and a set of case recordings; and

    f) the assessor report.

3. The assessment process should be recorded in a learning agreement and include a professional development plan with provision for appropriate reviews.

4. The process of confirming assessment will include internal and external moderation to confirm the assessment outcomes:

    a) Internal moderation: to confirm the assessment decision;

    b) External Moderation: to ensure the standards are consistently applied, through sampling assessment decisions and providing feedback to employers; and

    c) National validation: to show how the systems and processes which underpin the ASYE programme enable Newly Qualified Social Workers to reach the appropriate standard; and to ensure these standards are consistently applied.

Appendix 3: Honey and Mumford's learning styles

(Honey and Mumford, 1992)

Type	Learn most from and motivated by	Particularly like	Learn least from	Particularly dislike
Activists	• new experiences, problems or opportunities • short spontaneous exercises, tasks and games • excitement, drama, crisis and a variety of diverse activities • being in the 'limelight', including chairing, leading and presenting • being allowed to generate ideas without the constraints of practicality, policy or resource implications • being involved in a difficult task • being involved with others • having a go (trying something for the first time)	• participating in new or novel experiences • tackling real problems • activities relating to future roles	• taking a passive role, being asked to stand back and not get involved • assimilating and analysing data • working on their own • being asked, before the learning event, to identify what they will learn and after the event, to appraise what they have learned • being too theoretical • being involved in repetitive activities • being asked to carry out instructions with little room for manoeuvre • being meticulous to detail	• formulating objectives • clarifying • regularity • imposed structure • direct teaching inputs where they are expected to be passive or to sit on the sidelines

Type	Learn most from and motivated by	Particularly like	Learn least from	Particularly dislike
Reflectors	• being able to stand back, listen to and observe what is going on • thinking before acting, having time to prepare • carrying out research where they can investigate and assemble ideas • reviewing what has happened and what they have learned • being asked to produce carefully considered analyses • exchanging views with other people in a safe, structured environment • reaching decisions in their own time, without pressure and tight deadlines	• observing someone else • the opportunity to plan before action • the opportunity to analyse • reviewing • thinking things over • giving and getting feedback • receiving help from others	• being forced into the limelight, to take a lead • situations which require action without planning • short notice of an event they have to organise • being given insufficient data on which to base a conclusion • being given exact instructions of how things should be done • being pressurised by time limits or rushed from one activity to the next • having to take short cuts or do a superficial job	• performing without preparation
Theorists	• being offered (part of) a system, model, concept or theory • having time to explore associations and inter-relationships between ideas, events and situations	• a carefully prepared session • situations where participation is structured	• doing something without a context or apparent purpose • situations which emphasise emotions or feelings	• concentrating on one particular problem • the absence of a process of generalisation

Type	Learn most from and motivated by	Particularly like	Learn least from	Particularly dislike
	• having the opportunity to question the rationale or logic behind something • being pushed intellectually • structured situations with a clear purpose • ideas and concepts that emphasise rationality and logic (even if they do not appear immediately relevant) • being asked to analyse before being asked to generalise • attempting to understand complex situations	• intellectual activities • considering the theory behind something	• unstructured activities and open-ended problem solving • being asked to decide something without consideration to policy, principle or concept • exploring something only superficially • subject matter which is not statistically validated, has unsound methodology, is insufficient in evidence to support arguments • situations where they feel different from the other learners	• activities which encourage ambiguity and uncertainty • ad hoc sessions
Pragmatists	• an obvious link between the subject matter and a problem • techniques for doing things with obvious practical advantages (eg how to save time, revise better, etc.)	• situations where the learning activity is not seen to be related to a recognisable, immediate, practical benefit	• situations where there is not practice or clear guidelines on how to do a task	• moving outside their present role • an absence of any link to reality

Type	Learn most from and motivated by	Particularly like	Learn least from	Particularly dislike
	• an opportunity to try out and practise and get feedback from a person they consider to be a good practitioner themselves • a model which they can emulate • situations where they can see that what they are doing is applicable to their job situation • immediate implementation of what they have learned • Concentration on practical issues (eg actions, plans, recommendations)	• teachers who seem distant from reality	• situations where they cannot implement what they are learning • situations where there is no apparent reward for the learning activity	

Appendix 4: Time management exercise

As a first stage in practising organising your time, draw yourself a chart for the next week. Block out times for study, times for work, times for home duties and times for leisure/social activities. In each block, write the activities that you intend to undertake at this time, and any resources you will need or people you need to involve which will need planning in advance. Show where this advance planning will take place.

Although you will not want to plan with this level of detail all the time, it should help you to realise how useful it can be to plan ahead.

	Mon	Tues	Wed	Thurs	Fri	Sat	Sun
7am–12pm							
12pm–5pm							
5pm–10pm							
10pm–2am							
2am–7am							

Appendix 5: Reflective activities and tools

Reflective log template

Date of learning event

About me

My experience of the subject prior to the learning event

Facts

How was the learning acquired? (eg lecture, work with service user, team meeting)	What was the subject or topic of the learning event?
What happened during the learning event?	Which part of the event was most significant and/or important to you?

Feelings

What aspect of the event went well?	What was not so good?
What were your feelings about what happened?	What do you think others were feeling? (if appropriate)

Learning

What were your desired learning outcomes?	Where does it link in with, expand or complement your existing knowledge or skill?
What have you learned from the event?	

Conclusions

What do you need to do next?	How can you put your learning into practice in another situation?

SWOT analysis

The following questions might help you to focus your thinking and therefore your learning.

Strengths (Current)	Weaknesses (Current)
What do you consider you do well? What do you consider your greatest strength to be? What do you think other people see as your strengths? What has been your major achievement in your current role? What knowledge or skill can you share with others? Under what circumstances do you learn or develop most effectively?	What skills or knowledge do you think you could improve? What weaknesses have other people observed and pointed out to you? What feedback have you been given about areas you might want to develop? Under what circumstances do you find it most difficult to learn?
Opportunities (Future)	**Threats (Future)**
Do you know what you will need to carry out your role in the immediate or medium term? What resources will you need to help you to improve your identified areas of weakness? How can you try to make sure the resources are available? Where can you get help for things that concern you? What opportunities are there for you to build on your strengths? What method(s) would you choose for your own development?	Do you have any personal issues or barriers which could stop you from developing? Can you anticipate events which might prove a barrier to you developing? Are you able to reflect accurately and honestly on your development? Are you realistic about your capabilities?

Critical incidents

The following table gives some suggestions about questions that you might ask yourself as a starting point. You may want to use this table as a reference point as you go through the rest of this appendix, where we will suggest you work through a specific critical incident and record your analysis of it.

Stages	Questions to ask	People involved
Descriptive	What happened?	Who was involved?
	What made it happen?	Who acted?
Diagnostic	What does it do?	For whom?
	What does it feel like?	For whom?
	What does it mean?	To whom?
	Why does (did) it occur?	With whom?
Reflective	Do I like it? Is it a good thing? Why?	Do others like it? How does it affect them?
	What is it an example of?	Whose classification?
Critical	Is it just?	For whom?
Practical	What should I do? How? When? Where?	For and/or with whom?

Critical incident template

What happened?

Questions to ask yourself	Your record
What did you read, see, hear of what happened? What was the context? What were the main points, or stages, in what order, when? Did one thing follow from another? What were you responsible for?	

Questions to ask yourself	Your record
What other information would help you describe the experience, eg how long did it take; who else was involved; what costs were involved? Are other people's views relevant? What were they?	

How did you feel?

Questions to ask yourself	Your record
What was your initial gut feeling? What does that tell you? What were your subsequent feelings? What do they tell you?	

How did others react?

Questions to ask yourself	Your record
Did others react like you? Did they react differently? How? Who reacted in the same way? Who reacted differently? What does this suggest?	

What was good?

Questions to ask yourself	Your record
What pleased/interested you? What was good? Did you succeed in something difficult? What? How? Why? What/who was helpful? What points were made? What were your findings? What skills/qualities/abilities did you use? What was important to you?	

What needed improvement?

Questions to ask yourself	Your record
What made you unhappy/concerned? What was poor/didn't work well? Were there difficulties? Did you fail to do something? What/who was unhelpful? What needs improvement?	

What have you learned?

Questions to ask yourself	Your record
What were the main points to emerge from the detail? What common aspects are there between this and other experiences? What caused them?	
Were there any differences between this and other experiences? What caused them? Were your feelings similar to your feelings in other situations? Why did you feel like that? Why do you usually feel like that in such situations? Why do you think it was like that? What might happen in the future which could be the same? What would make it different? What if ...?	

Appendix 6: Developing, assessing and reviewing portfolios

What to do	How to do it	Who is involved
Develop a framework and documentation for portfolio.	Link the syllabus (if any) to the overall learning objectives of the learning programme, PCF, SoPs and any other relevant assessment frameworks. Differentiate between the essential and the desirable outcomes. Write appropriate guidance notes for learners, supervisors, assessors and other people involved. Devise appropriate forms/checklists, etc. that will be used for review and assessment.	Tutor, placement educator, team manager, supervisor, staff development officer.
Establish means for supporting the learner during portfolio development.	Identify educational supervisors and/or mentors. Implement training for those involved in providing support.	As above.
Introduce portfolio to learners.	Present and explain documentation or e-portfolio format – may be appropriately done during induction to learning programme or employment. Name individuals designated to support and review the portfolio.	As above.
Develop individual learning plan	Identify current level of learning in key areas for review – eg domains or levels of PCF.	Educational supervisor/tutor/employer and individual learner through negotiation.

What to do	How to do it	Who is involved
	Identify areas for future development. Agree key learning objectives, linking individual learning needs and relevant syllabus/ framework including PCF and SoPs. Agree means for meeting personal needs and objectives.	
Identify sources of evidence of learning appropriate to identified learning needs.	Agree which objectives may be met through natural work patterns, and which will need specific training input. Identify and arrange training where appropriate. Agree what types of evidence would be considered appropriate to demonstrate learning achievement.	Educational supervisor and learner.
Gather and document evidence of learning.	Ensure that appropriate evidence of learning is gathered and its rationale for inclusion in the portfolio is established. Supplement with reflective accounts of learning as appropriate.	Learner in collaboration with mentor/supervisor/ trainer if appropriate.
Monitor progress.	Review learning objectives and progress towards their attainment. Ensure evidence relates to and demonstrates how learning objectives have been addressed. Revise learning objectives if necessary.	Learner with mentor and/ or supervisor/manager.

What to do	How to do it	Who is involved
Assess/review portfolio.	Select and provide rationale for evidence that demonstrates achievement of learning objectives under review.	Learner. Learner with reviewer/assessor. Reviewer/assessor.
	Ensure validity, sufficiency, authenticity of evidence and currency of learning.	Learner with reviewer/assessor. Learner with reviewer/assessor.
	Agree whether evidence meets defined assessment criteria.	
	Plan further learning opportunities if necessary.	
	Devise new learning objectives and personal learning plan.	
Report results to appropriate bodies.	Complete documentation. Make recommendations for progression/additional support needed.	Learner/supervisor/tutor/HCPC.

Index

Page numbers in *italics* refer to figures.